ELDER ABUSE

YOU HAVE A ROLE TO PLAY

START THE CONVERSATION **NOW**
TO PROTECT THE ONES WE LOVE

JOHN E. JOHNSON &
SABBY DUTHIE

Elder Abuse - You Have A Role To Play Copyright © 2021 by John E. Johnson and Sabby Duthie.

All rights reserved. No part of this publication may be reproduced, distributed or transmitted in any form or by any means, including photocopying, recording, or other electronic or mechanical methods, without the prior written permission of the publisher, except in the case of brief quotations embodied in critical reviews and certain other noncommercial uses permitted by copyright law.

All net proceeds of the sale of each book will be distributed by BridgeGen Canada Centre, a non-profit organization, to groups supporting the fight against ageism and elder abuse.

Prominence Publishing
www.prominencepublishing.com

Elder Abuse - You Have A Role To Play/ John E. Johnson and Sabby Duthie -- 1st ed.

ISBN: 978-1-988925-73-8

Table of Contents

Introduction 1
Information You Need About Elder Abuse 3
Chapter 1: Physical Abuse 5
Chapter 2: Sexual Abuse 11
Chapter 3: Psychological Abuse 17
Chapter 4: Neglect 23
Chapter 5: Financial Abuse.. 29
Chapter 6: Institutional Elder Abuse 35
Chapter 7: Aging At Home 51
Chapter 8: Elder Abuse and Culture 57
Chapter 9: The Community - Who Can I Trust? 69
Chapter 10: You Must Use Your Voice 81
Chapter 11: What Makes Us Think The Way We Do? 87
Chapter 12: We All Have a Role to Play 93
About the Authors 99
Resources & Helplines 107

Introduction

Statistics tell us that seven out of ten incidents of abuse are never reported to anyone. We have gathered data from recognized experts to provide you with the proof that abuse of senior citizens is real, and it is widespread. This is why it is important for you to read this book. As more people read this book and become intrigued with elder abuse, then we will all work together to find the right solution to deal with this growing problem in our society.

Both Sabby and I have had first-hand experience in the world of elder abuse. Sabby as a former retirement home owner and I as a lawyer with 40 years of experience in both exposing and stopping abuse in the courts.

To get your attention we have assembled anecdotal evidence from our own experience in order to provide you with guidance to prevent our seniors from being harmed or to stop the harm before any serious damage is done.

The patterns of abuse that we experienced repeat themselves over and over again with the same predictable results. Unless action is taken to intervene when the pattern is observed, the abuse will continue and repeat itself.

We are just as certain that we cannot do this by ourselves. We need an entire community to prevent, intervene, and stop elder abuse. We believe that a conscientious and empathetic observer of human nature will have all the tools needed to recognize elder abuse in its early stages and take the necessary steps to protect those who have spent their lifetimes protecting us.

Information You Need About Elder Abuse

Elder abuse is defined by the World Health Organization (WHO) as "a single or repeated act or lack of appropriate action occurring within any relationship where there is an expectation of trust which causes harm or distress to an older person."[1]

As the prevalence of elder abuse grew it became evident that proof was needed of the size and nature of it. One of the longest studies of a single community was conducted by the National Initiative for the Care of the Elderly. Two years in the making it was published in 2015 under the acronym of NICE.

We have relied on the statistical results of the survey and are comforted that there was nothing in our own experience that caused us to think differently and it supported our need to look at solutions.

The national survey on the mistreatment of older Canadians 2015, the NICE survey revealed the following:

> The aggregate prevalence for physical, sexual, psychological, financial abuse and neglect was 8.2% representing 766,247 older Canadians. What this means is that 8.2% of older Canadians over 55 years of age have been exposed to some form of abuse or mistreatment.

Through the use of stories that are based on the events from our own experience, we shall examine the various types of abuse or neglect that illustrate solutions for the early remediation of the problems in each area of abuse. We have changed the names and facts slightly to protect the identities of the people whose stories are being told.

Chapter 1: Physical Abuse

There are basically five different kinds of elder abuse. Physical abuse, sexual abuse, neglect, psychological abuse, and financial abuse. Each of these will be dealt with separately in the chapters that follow.

A Story of Physical Abuse

Physical abuse often includes financial abuse because the two are frequently intertwined, as you will see. The main actors here are Mrs. Green and her son, who we will call Junior. It is my intent to show that physical abuse will more often occur if only the abuser and the victim are present.

Mrs. Green was 82 years old. She owned the house in which she was living, free and clear. Her husband had died five years prior and both she and her husband had government pensions which she now survived on, alongside CPP and OAS.

There were several brothers and sisters in this family and when one of her bachelor sons stepped forward offering to care for his mother, the family acquiesced, despite knowing that he had a sporadic work history and lived on welfare from the Regional Municipality. The other siblings were busy, successful people so they thought this could work, and in any event, none of them were keen to step forward.

A female housekeeper, Mrs. Juarez, was also hired to keep the place clean and attend to Mrs. Green's personal needs. Junior, who it seemed should have appreciated his good fortune, was asked by the welfare folks to provide proof that he was paying rent to his mother. So he made cheques to Mrs. Green for $500 a month and deposited them into her bank account. This arrangement seemed to be common knowledge within the family and Mrs. Green did not complain because Junior had graciously agreed to help her manage her accounts, which to anyone's knowledge had about $250,000 in them (plus, of course, the $500 per month Junior gave her).

Junior never had it so good. Junior bought himself a Chrysler and to give his mother some time off, he disappeared on the weekends. Later as it turned out, it was to a cottage he had purchased on a nice local lake where he fished from his 60 hp motorboat.

Junior also used his mother's money to buy a condominium in Florida to which he escaped to avoid the cold for three months every winter. He never invited his mother to join him.

Junior continued to pay rent to his mother just as everyone had agreed. After two or three years of this routine, there came a day when it was raining outside. The housekeeper was on her way home for the day, but she had forgotten her umbrella and went back to the house. She heard screaming and yelling from both Mrs. Green and her son. Hidden from sight, the housekeeper saw Junior hit his mother with his fist, leaving bruises on her upper arm and ligature marks on her wrists where Junior had tied his mother to her wheelchair. Mrs. Green was apparently objecting to giving out any more money to her son. Junior had also hit her on the head. Mrs. Green had always denied that the marks on her person were any fault but her own. The housekeeper sneaked out and called the eldest brother who called the police.

Junior was charged with assault and breach of trust. The Regional Municipality sought a restitution order for $36,000 for his fake claim for welfare monies and the family was able to recover the cottage, boat, Chrysler, and the condo.

Junior cooperated with all the paperwork and bawled his eyes out in court, saying he was the only one who really cared for her. He got two years in jail. For her part, Mrs.

Green was restored her lost money and cut Junior out of her will.

Following the NICE findings, 207,889 of 766,247 or 2.2% of the older Canadians studied, suffered physical abuse at the hands of another. The perpetrator was seen to be as follows:

Physical Abuser	Percentage of Group
Spouse/ex-spouse	34
Adult Child or Grandchild	27
Friend	12
Service Provider	7
Someone at Work	7
Sibling	4
Neighbour or Acquaintance	4
Stranger	3
Other	2

The Epilogue

This true story went forward innocently enough at the beginning and is very typical. Junior was the only family member to volunteer for a job nobody really wanted. He needed a place to live and some extra money for things he could never afford.

Initially, Mrs. Green was happy because she now had the company of a family member and her son could help her with financial matters under the power of attorney. Her wheelchair was always a real obstacle for her.

Remember that 91% of abusers are known to the victim. Junior was an excellent example of this kind of abuser. This means that they are not usually professional criminals, but they are usually unsuccessful in their financial and social achievements and cowards of the highest order. Once exposed, Junior was easy to extricate from the scene. The key in this case was the interference of the witness, Mrs. Juarez. The housekeeper interrupted the privacy of Junior and exposed his actions. He could not continue to beat his mother in the presence of a witness and his fraudulent actions could not continue once the family had knowledge of them.

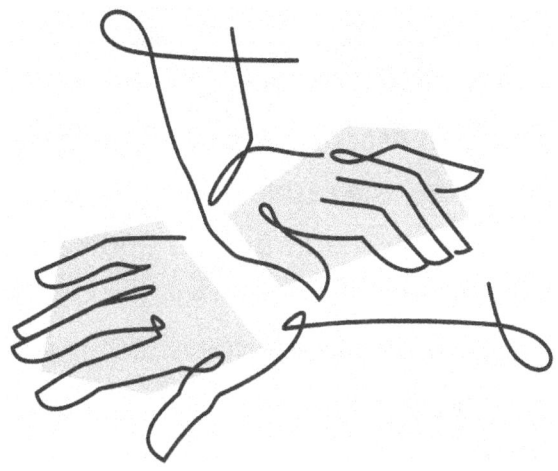

Chapter 2: Sexual Abuse

A Story of Sexual Abuse

This story opens up with Susan and Mark and shows how the institutional audience, the retirement home, in this case, has the power to help and they do.

Susan and Mark have been married for over 50 years and have decided that it is time to move out of their matrimonial home and into a retirement home. Both Susan and Mark are physically well, but Mark has dementia and although it is manageable, his mental health is declining. Mark has had a very gentle nature all his life, understanding and very respectful towards Susan during their marriage. He held a very respectable position as Chief Operating Officer of a large company and happily provided well for his wife, and two daughters.

Susan and Mark settled in comfortably to their retirement home living. It was a year later that Susan noticed a change in Mark's behaviour. He began to joke a lot with the other female residents and the staff. His joking, however, was sexually inappropriate and he also began to provide unwanted hugs to other residents. One day, while in the elevator, Susan noticed that another elderly female resident (we shall call her Jane) was reluctant to share the elevator with her and Mark. Over the next few weeks, Susan continued to notice that Jane was often uncomfortable and agitated when she or Mark approached her personal space. Jane no longer came to social activities and refused to play Bridge with Susan.

Susan realized something was not right, but she was in a very difficult position. Mark, her husband of fifty years, whom she loved dearly, was no longer the person that she had known because of his dementia. He would never have condoned inappropriate sexual behaviour, yet he was now participating in it himself.

Susan strongly suspected that Jane was also suffering and required help. Susan decided that she needed to do something and brought this situation to the head of the nursing department. The head of nursing thanked Susan and assured her that the proper help and support would be provided to her husband and to Jane. The head of nursing investigated the matter and found that Mark had been visiting Jane in secret and would give her unwanted hugs, touch her legs and face and discuss at length his sexual desires. The head of nursing shared these findings with Susan. Together with the help of the retirement home, Mark was able to get the help and support that he required, and Jane got the help that she needed.

The NICE survey revealed that 146,649 of 766,247 or 1.6% of the older Canadians studied suffered incidents of sexual abuse at the hands of another. The perpetrator was seen to be as follows:

Sexual Abuser	Percentage of Group
Spouse/ex-spouse	19
Friend	50
Service Provider	9
Someone at Work	11
Neighbour or Acquaintance	2
Stranger	7
Other	2

The Epilogue

Those seniors who have been subjected to sexual abuse are unlikely to report it because of fear or shame. There are seniors who are unable to communicate and seek help because of their own mental health or dementia. It is important to ask questions when one notices bruises around the breast and genitals, unexplained vaginal or anal bleeding, or torn, stained, or bloody underclothing. Ask more questions when a senior's behaviour changes and becomes more agitated; socially and emotionally withdrawn or flinches when an unwanted person comes close to them. In our story, Susan saw what was happening and was courageous enough to bring it to the attention of the people who could help.

Sexual abuse amongst our seniors is very prevalent. Not only is it the most hidden form of elder abuse, it is also the least acknowledged by family and seldom reported. The stereotype that an older person is no longer a sexual being is wrong. This helps keep the sexual abuse of the older person hidden and because it is not discussed much, it is an abuse that is growing amongst seniors in our society.

Sexual abuse is non-consensual sexual contact of any kind. Sexual contact with any person who is incapable of giving consent is sexual abuse. Examples of sexual abuse are rape, showing pornographic materials, forcing the older person to watch sexual acts, forcing them to undress, or any form of unwanted touching or comments.

In this case, Mark's wife had to make a very difficult decision. But by reaching out for help, she was able to get the support that *she* needed, the support that *Jane* needed and the help that *Mark* required. The role that the retirement home played was critical, since they were in a very strong position to understand what Mark, Jane, and Susan were each going through. Because of that understanding, they were able to get the right help for everyone.

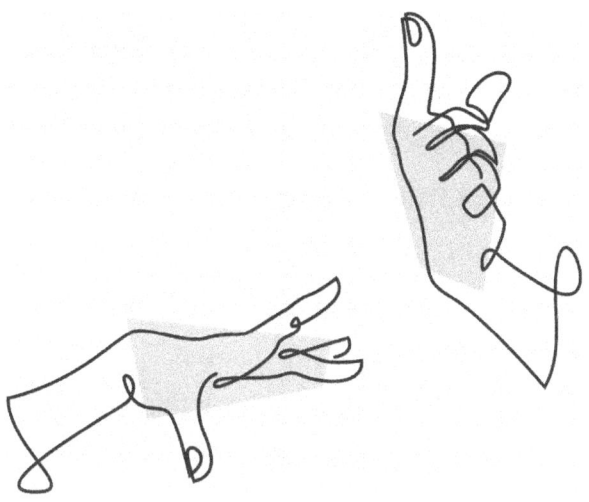

Chapter 3: Psychological Abuse

A Story of Psychological Abuse

This next story did not come from my file drawer, but was told to me by a nurse. A daughter had brought her 80-year-old father to the doctor's office because the daughter alleged that her father had become demented. The doctor's record showed that he presented as anxious and depressed and was apprehensive as to what was going to happen to him. His daughter had told him she had brought him so he could be committed and she would not have to look after him anymore.

The father was undernourished and lacking in proper hygiene. He told the doctor that his daughter was giving him sleeping pills, so she would not have to look after him when she went out. The daughter had told him that if he did not go with her to the doctor, she would put him in an institution. She threatened him with this all the time and said it was because he was crazy. The doctor's record showed that the father was quite sad at his predicament, but otherwise a very astute and intelligent elderly man, who had been browbeaten endlessly with statements like, "Why can't you just die like ordinary people?"

The doctor called the Public Guardian to investigate. The father was placed in protection with no contact with the daughter.

The NICE survey revealed not unexpectedly that psychological abuse is very much the product of family discord. The prevalence of psychological abuse was found by NICE to be 2.7% representing 251,157 Canadians.

Psychological Abuser	Percentage of Group
Spouse/ex-spouse	41
Adult Children	25
Friend	12
Siblings	9
Service Provider	4
Someone at Work	6
Neighbour or Acquaintance	1
Other	2

The Epilogue

Psychological abuse often accompanies physical abuse and will usually include willful or reckless verbal or non-verbal infliction of emotional or mental anguish and the use of physical or chemical restraint or medication or isolation as a punishment.

As you can imagine, this comes in many forms but here is a short list: lying to the individual senior, hiding his or her belongings, humiliating or infantilizing, inappropriate shouting or yelling, controlling contact with people, social isolation from family or friends, threatening to hit or throw something, talking disrespectfully, not respecting privacy, threatening to have him or her declared incompetent and put in an asylum.[2] An elderly person who has been psychologically abused will often present as apprehensive, passive, quiet, withdrawn. Sometimes your reception by the
elder person will be angry and resentful because they fear the consequences of being found out.

Quite often, the abuser adopts the role of caregiver and their goal is to isolate the senior from all persons familiar to him or her, and any form of activity that could provide comfort to the senior person, who in most instances is residing in his or her own home. A simple but common example is the relocation of the residential telephone to make it more "convenient" to everybody in the house. The phone is placed out of reach to a seated person, with a call display installed so that the abuser can reach the phone first and restrict phone calls to the senior person. If calls are permitted, they have to be taken in the living room so the victim can be monitored. If the abuser answers the phone, the abuser will report who has and has not called and announce, "Nobody ever calls for you. I am the only one who cares what happens to you. If it were not for me, you would have to go to an institution."

Over the years, in reflecting upon the various kinds of abuse, I think that the presence of psychological abuse appeared as part of the pattern of elder abuse in every case. Quite often the relationships of the parties were long-standing. It seemed that to some extent the older person accepted some responsibility for their own treatment. Often, this was because they were embarrassed at the social predicament of their adult child, whose life had not turned out the way that either expected due to illness, mental or physical problems, the effects of alcohol or drugs, or some other disability. Other causes I often witnessed involved the death or divorce of a spouse of either the victim or the abuser.

Their circumstances have brought them to the same place to live together, usually the residence of the abused person and probably the family home.

Each will have their own reasons why they have been brought together. Their situation is often of long duration, especially where the victim and abuser are both women because the spectre of physical violence is less present, but the verbal and psychological interface continues.

A typical dispute revolves around the work involved in looking after the physical needs of an older person and having to contend with taking them to appointments. Unfortunately, the older person feels their frailties as much as the abuser. Battles continue and while the social system of assistance is often available to meet their needs, it is not always used.

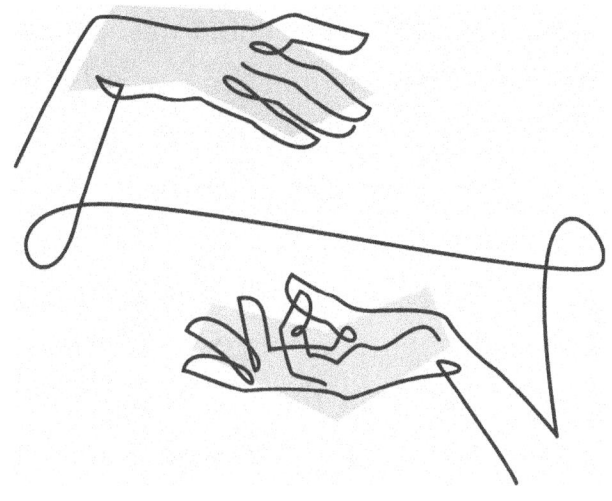

Chapter 4: Neglect

A Story of Neglect

In one of my cases, there were two daughters. Their mother and father lived together in anything but harmony. Seizing the moment, one of the daughters took her mother to a lawyer to get papers drawn up for a divorce. The mother bought into the program, divorced the father, and divided the matrimonial property. The daughter then took her mother 300 miles away to live at a lakeside cottage that was 20 miles from the highway.

The mother gave her daughter a power of attorney for personal care and property and rewrote her will, leaving her whole estate to her "devoted daughter". The daughter decided to celebrate and took a 12-week cruise through the

Panama Canal, something she could never have afforded on her part-time employment at the grocery store.

While she was away, a friend offered to look in on the mother now and then. Other than these short and infrequent visits, the mother was alone in the bush.

Tragically, the daughter died on-board the ship and the friend looking in on her mother also fell ill. Luckily, the friend had enough sense to tell the OPP about the mother's situation and they were able to go in and rescue her. When they found her, she was without suitable food or clothing and living in filthy conditions.

Both the father and the other daughter were relieved to find the mother safe and sound, as they had no idea where the deceased sister had been keeping her. They found a lovely placement in a long-term care centre where the mother was diagnosed with a very violent form of dementia due in large part to her ordeal with the daughter who had taken her away.

The NICE survey revealed that 116,256 of 766,247 or 1.2% of the older Canadians studied suffered incidents of neglect at the hands of another. The perpetrator was seen to be as follows:

Neglect Perpetrator	Percentage of Group
Spouse/ex-spouse	31
Adult Child or Grandchild	25
Friends	11
Caregivers	9
Siblings	5
Neighbour or Acquaintance	14
Service Providers	3
Other	2

The Epilogue

In this story, the parents were both wealthier than their children — one daughter was fully functional as a self-employed businesswoman and the other was a grocery clerk. The plan of the poor daughter was to take over the role of caregiver and companion for her mother, who was more sympathetic to her needs. The opinion of the father that this daughter was a no-good, lazy, useless person did not help his cause. His attitude ignited a very expensive experience for him in the courts, while his daughter took over her mother's case. Although this could have been brought to rest by family counselling or some other form of intervention, the mother supported the enterprise due to her own dislike of her husband and his dislike of the unsuccessful daughter.

The daughter moved with great speed to alienate her mother from all social contact and to place her in a remote location, which was unfit and far removed from the lifestyle her mother had previously enjoyed.

As soon as her mother was under control without contact with anyone, the daughter took some money and went away, leaving her mother with a friend to look in on her. Earlier intervention with this chain of events might have saved the mother from her imprisonment by breaking the connection.

I believe that once the father discovered the path of destruction and evil bestowed upon his former wife by the daughter, he went out of his way to restore the relationship with his wife. Unfortunately, it was too late.

The daughter failed to provide the care and assistance required for her mother's safety and well-being. Her acts of neglect were deliberate. She needed to control her mother and to do so she needed to take over control of her assets.

Another scenario for neglect finds the elderly person in need of some assistance to enable her continuing occupation of her home. A volunteer usually a family member, moves into the residence as a "caregiver." After a few months, a visual inspection reveals unsanitary living conditions. Proper meals are not being prepared and bedding is not being changed. The "caregiver" is often out doing "errands" and has the older person's vehicle and the use of a bank or credit card. The senior will often be found alone with means of contact with others taken away. Access to health aids such as glasses, hearing aids, walkers and wheelchairs are taken away or hidden. The senior's prescriptions are nowhere to be found, but a large bottle of sleeping pills is in the medicine cabinet.

Further investigations will reveal that if and when the senior person requires medical treatment, the "caregiver" will insist on being present during the appointment and will try to control the conversation with the nurse or doctor to explain the obvious decline in the senior's health or any bruises cuts or burns which may appear. Many times, the senior will concur to avoid controversy.

The "caregiver" will feign dissatisfaction with the current doctor and seek to change to another doctor, so the neglect will go unnoticed. Follow-up will be made very difficult and the well-being of the elderly person will decline both mentally and physically. Visitors will be discouraged so these conditions remain a secret.

What is really required, is to ensure that the visits to the residence of the older person are regular, with records kept of conversations with both the senior and the alleged "caregiver" — for later use in reporting matters, as required.

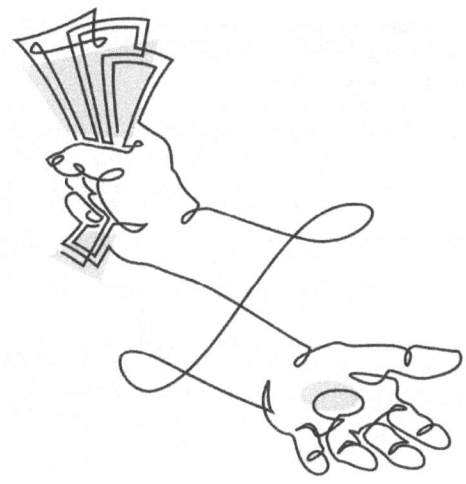

Chapter 5: Financial Abuse

A Story of Financial Abuse

In this next case, the mother, Mrs. Smith, had a Ph.D. in Science and was as astute as you could imagine with her finances, as she had previously managed them with her deceased husband, another scientist. The couple had four sons and one daughter. Each of the sons had all the education they needed to be successful and had moved to other large cities across Canada. The daughter stayed in the small town where she had grown up with her parents and brothers. It seemed only logical that the daughter would help her mother to look after her affairs when she began to go blind from macular degeneration. All the paperwork was done, and the daughter took over control of her affairs. They would meet often to discuss her mother's investments and they got along just fine with no evidence of any form of abuse.

The daughter had three girls and was married to a bus driver. One day, the local bank manager called Mrs. Smith and told her she was overdrawn on her chequing account. The bank manager explained that there had been several large withdrawals in the last two years and that he had been meaning to call her. Mrs. Smith arranged a meeting with one of her sons and they discovered the disappearance of $750,000, all under the signature of her daughter. She admitted everything when confronted and an order was obtained to freeze all of her assets and to return them to her mother.

I asked the daughter why she had done this, and she said that her brothers had all the advantages and she had nothing and was left looking after her mother. Mrs. Smith insisted that no charges be laid to protect her granddaughters. The assets were almost all recovered except for the granddaughters' private school fees. The daughter had to return the $500,000 house six doors down from her mother, who never even knew she lived there.

It would be rare in my experience for elder abuse, in the form of physical abuse, psychological abuse or neglect, to manifest without there being a plan for the improper taking, misuse or concealment of the resources or property or other assets of a senior person.

In more general terms, financial abuse can be described as the deprivation or exploitation of a person's property by fraudulent means.

The following are suggestive of financial or material abuse[3]:

1. Use of bank accounts, money or credit/debit cards against the individual's will, with or without his or her knowledge.

2. An individual is forced to give a power of attorney.

3. Cashed cheques or property sold, and the money kept.

4. Forged signatures.

5. Individuals are forced to sign documents against their will or understanding.

6. Misinformation about funds.

7. Misappropriation of funds, property, or power of attorney for personal gain.

The previous forms of abuse are often part of the plan to take over the elder person's money and other property. Financial abuse can stand alone. Often the elder person is a willing participant because of a family relationship with their abuser.

The NICE survey determined that financial abuse was largely a family matter. The prevalence of Financial Abuse is 2.6% representing 244,176 Canadians.

Financial Abuser	Percentage of Group
Spouse/ex-spouse	22
Adult Child or Grandchild	37
Friends	8
Service Providers	4
Siblings	15
Neighbour or Acquaintance	3
Strangers	10
Other	1

The Epilogue

This story demonstrates the opposite end of the spectrum of financial abuse. When the father died he left an estate in excess of five million dollars. Both seniors were astute money managers and their financial plans were put in place long before the mother started to go blind. The daughter was close to her mother and in a small town, this was well known. The woman's sons were not very attentive but visited from time to time and there was no lack of contact with their mother.

In the making of her will, the mother divided the estate equally. Her children all knew that this was the case and no one had dared take issue with her as she was quite determined in her ways. The daughter had initially accepted that her mother was unmoved on the subject but opportunity knocked when the mother became blind and the power of attorney for the property was invoked so that the daughter could now take care of the finances, but always under her mother's instructions. The situation at the bank just became a de facto changing of the guard, so that the daughter had complete control and her mother trusted her explicitly until the money that was in the account ran out. It was the banker who advised the mother that she had bounced a cheque and that her account, which formerly had a large amount of money in it, was now empty.

Who is to blame for the debacle? Some of the blame has to be with the victim who was not careful enough to put in place protection and oversight. From the information I had, the mother was very independent. Her sons should also have been invited to these family conversations.

The mother needed more planning and more transparency. She also needed to think about a separate allocation to help her daughter who had been a long and faithful supporter of her needs. It was too much to resist for the daughter. She should have asked her brothers to talk to the mother about compensation, before defrauding her mother in such a bold way. In the end, justice was served as the mother cut the daughter out of the will before she died.

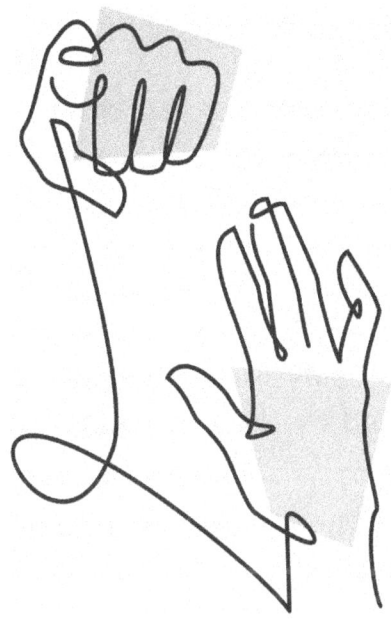

Chapter 6: Institutional Elder Abuse

The abuse in an institutional setting can be placed into the following categories:

1. Resident to Resident abuse.

2. Worker to Resident abuse.

3. Visitor to Resident abuse.

It is already challenging for an older person to move from their home into an institutional setting. So to surround them with the potential threat of elder abuse in these settings is truly not acceptable. Let us look at the following stories and see what role the institutional community can play in addressing elder abuse.

A Story of Resident to Resident Abuse

Vivian Smith moved into a retirement home six months ago and was so excited about the move. She had spent a considerable amount of time searching for the perfect retirement home and she finally felt that she had found the right one. The staff at the retirement home were very pleasant, and during her visit, she enjoyed a beautiful meal and was welcomed by the residents. The residents spoke very highly of the home and the management. Vivian's time at the retirement home was very enjoyable. She would attend bridge and exercise classes regularly. She was a great person to have at social events since she would also engage in interesting conversations with other residents and guests. At mealtimes, the other residents enjoyed her company because she always knew how to see the positive side of every conversation.

However, this has changed recently. Vivian does not attend bridge or exercise classes and she is extremely quiet at social events and mealtimes. A new resident, Jane, moved in a few months ago. Jane has been very rude towards Vivian. Jane comments on how Vivian dresses, on how she walks and on how she talks. Vivian did not think much of this and just ignored Jane, but now Jane's comments are beginning to hurt. Jane has recently told Vivian that everyone may be pleasant to her, but everyone laughs behind her back because of the way she walks and talks. Jane clearly told Vivian that no one really enjoys her conversations.

Vivian decided to speak about Jane's comments to the activity director and she assured her that this is not the case, since the other residents enjoy her company very much and no one had made any remarks about her at all. Vivian, then spoke to another resident and she provided the same advice. However, Jane continues to advise Vivian that no one likes her. She also tells her that her laugh is annoying and the other residents at the dinner table laugh at her because of the awful mess that she makes when she eats.

Over time, Jane's comments take a toll on Vivian. Vivian has stopped going to activities and stays more and more in her room. She even prefers to eat in her own room as opposed to the dining room. She has not participated in her daily exercises and she is finding that the lack of exercise is taking a toll on her walking. Over time, Vivian's mental and physical health deteriorates.

The Epilogue

What could the institutional facility have done in Vivian's case?

Resident to resident abuse does exist in institutions. Jane is bullying Vivian and her behaviour is having a negative impact on Vivian, both emotionally and physically. The institutional facility could have considered taking the following steps:

1. The retirement home knew of Vivian's personality, her behaviour, and her routine. Any change in her personality and her routine should have been investigated. If she was not attending activities that she used to attend, then the question should have been raised as to why? This would then have prompted further investigation.

2. Vivian took the initiative to reach out for help. When Vivian went to the activity director to ask questions herself, the activity director did not take the time to acknowledge Vivian's pain. Instead, she ignored it. She should have then discussed Vivian's situation with the rest of her management team so that they were on alert and if an opportunity presented itself for them to intervene, then the cycle of abuse that Vivian endured would have ended. Teaching staff about what to look for, how to respond, and how to work as a team to address elder abuse, is training that cannot just be offered on the first day of work. This training should be ongoing. Visible notices should be posted in the staff room that this is an 'elder abuse free zone.' Creating a culture and environment where elder abuse does not rear its ugly head, can only be done by acknowledging and understanding what elder abuse is

and creating a comfortable environment where elder abuse is openly discussed. Once that discussion has taken place, then it is much easier to look for solutions to address the problem.

3. Vivian did continue to seek for help. She turned to another resident and asked general questions. I understand that it is hard for other residents to be able to provide the support that Vivian needed; however, it is important to provide education to residents of the institutional facility on what elder abuse is and teach them that this behaviour will not be tolerated. Treating other residents with respect and dignity fosters a healthy environment that should be encouraged.

4. The institutional facilities are in a position of power to create a positive and loving atmosphere in their facilities. Creating a positive environment is a silent tool that fights away negative behaviour such as elder abuse. The family of each resident also has a role to play and the institutional facilities must include them as active members in the management of their institutional facility. They should include the family members in educational discussions on elder abuse, include the family in activities, and provide the family with the voice to offer suggestions on how the institutional facility can be a safe place for everyone.

5. Jane, in this case, is the abuser. It is important to provide immediate support to the person being abused; however, when the abuser is an older person, we cannot forget that the abuser will also need help. There may be other medical concerns that have arisen with the abuser that may explain the abuse, and if this is the case, then we must provide the support, compassion and care that the abuser requires. The institutional facility is in an excellent position to see this and provide the required support. The role of the medical community would be essential here. The nursing staff and the doctor should take time and provide the support that Vivian requires, but also take the time to question Jane's behaviour and see if there are any underlying medical concerns that need to be addressed.

A Story of Worker to Resident Abuse

Mary is a personal support worker and she enjoys providing care for the elderly. She has worked in long-term care for over five years. All the residents, staff, and family members truly love her. On her fifth work anniversary, she received beautiful thank you and congratulation cards from the residents and staff. However, what everyone sees about Mary is not the true picture. Behind closed doors, she befriends the residents and shares her own personal story of the difficulties that she is encountering at home. She obtains the trust of the residents and becomes their friend, rather than their caregiver. Over a period of time, the residents trust her. It is then that she starts to take the money that they offer. Mary is very intelligent, and she befriends everyone, but only takes money from those residents that have little or no friends or family. She knows that the chances of her "getting caught" are much smaller.

A Story of Visitors to Resident Abuse

James enjoys visiting with his father at the long-term care residence, and with Mr. Scott who lives next door to his father. Having a conversation with Mr. Scott is interesting since his cognition is very strong and Mr. Scott is so happy to have James visit, since he has no family and very few visitors. Over time, Mr. Scott starts to share more and more information about his personal life, especially his finances and the type of investments that he has made. James' father passes away, but James still continues to visit with Mr. Scott. Mr. Scott is honoured that James is still coming to visit him and begins to place more and more trust in James. One day, James brings forward an investment idea that he has been working on and shares his dream for building a restaurant. He asks Mr. Scott if he wants to be a part of this dream. Mr. Scott, who has become very fond of James, agrees to help. Over a period of one year, Mr. Scott has made an investment of over $250,000 into the restaurant. Then one day, James stops visiting Mr. Scott.

Mr. Scott becomes concerned and asks one of the staff members to look up the name of James' restaurant. She does and cannot locate one by that name. As more time passes with no visits from James, Mr. Scott realizes that the trust he had in James was not real and was just a ploy so that James could extract money from him.

The Epilogue

What could the institutional facility have done with respect to Mary's case and Mr. Scott's case?

The institutional facility has a role to play in safeguarding Mr. Scott and the residents that Mary took advantage of. The workers that work in institutional settings are our front-line workers who provide excellent care and support to the older person. It is also important to recognize that they are in a position of power, since the older person is relying on that worker to provide them with the care and services that they need on a daily basis. Visitors, be they family or friend, are also key individuals that provide the older person with much needed social interaction.

The community in an institutional setting is the resident, the family, the visitors, the caregivers, anyone else that enters into the institutional facility to provide support and assistance, and the staff, management and owners of the institutional facility. Acknowledgement and understanding need to be in place in the institutional setting that elder abuse does exist, and that it can exist in the homes that they own and operate. This acknowledgment alone is a critical step in addressing elder abuse. Acknowledgement that elder abuse can exist in a home puts into action education and no-tolerance for elder abuse.

Opening up conversation on elder abuse provides a safe and comfortable environment to discuss elder abuse, put in measures to address elder abuse and deters potential abusers. The institutional facility is in a position to play a stronger role to protect the ones that we love. They have the tools to educate, to put in place and conduct proper screening for workers and visitors to their facilities. When a case of elder abuse in an institutional facility is realized, we have the skilled professionals to provide the support to the abused and the abuser.

Institutionalized abuse is a growing concern

Elder abuse in an institutionalized setting is a growing concern and we believe it will become an even larger concern as our population ages, especially for those aged 80 and over. The United Nations predicts that the number of persons aged 80 years or over is projected to triple, from 143 million in 2019 to 426 million in 2050 and that 61.5% of those will be women.

Most of the older people who live in institutional settings have some form of impairment that puts them in a position where they are dependent on others for compassionate care and support. These older people are more at risk for elder abuse than their counterparts that are healthy, or living outside of an institutional setting.

We encourage our older person to report the abuse so that help can be provided. The reality, however, is that in institutional settings this may not be possible because the resident, who may have mental or physical impairments may not be able to communicate the abuse, or there may be a fear that if they report the abuse they will not receive the same level of care. The World Health Organization has stated that the prevalence of abuse may be much higher than reported since under-reporting is estimated to be as high as 80%.[4]

The right to a safe home

Creating and providing a positive home environment where one lives is one of the key cornerstones of living a healthy life. Your home is important to you, regardless of whether it is in an institutionalized setting or a home you own. Your home inspires you to exercise choice that promotes meaningful, positive, and active living, regardless of your age and health.

The basic tenets of providing a positive and inspiring housing environment should reinforce the following:

- Respecting the dignity and choice of the older person.

- Providing the older person with as much choice and access to active and healthy living as possible.

- Encouraging the older person to be as independent and involved in their decision making as possible.

- Respecting the individuality of the older person. It is only by recognizing our older person's individuality that we are able to appreciate the choices, the importance and value of independence.

- Respecting the role that family, friends, professionals and advisors, play in the life of the older person.

In a retirement home, the older person has the ability to move into a facility and have all the daily stresses of life looked after, such as housekeeping, meal preparation, and house maintenance. They are then able to concentrate on their own health. Long-term care facilities are there to ensure that our older person has a safe place to live and have their care needs looked after, in addition to these other services.

The benefits that these facilities offer are immense; however, it is important for these facilities to have the tools and measures in place to ensure that our older persons are looked after with respect, dignity and free from elder abuse. If these facilities fail to do that, then you can be assured that the seed of elder abuse will be planted, and will grow into a ravaging monster. The people that will pay the price will be our older members of society. The rest of us will simply be left to look on with shock.

As we were writing this chapter the world was experiencing the COVID-19 pandemic and the issue pertaining to the care of our older person in institutional settings was top of mind. Questions were being asked as to the care provided for the older person in some of these institutional settings. There were certainly grave examples where the care was not acceptable. COVID-19 clearly brought to light very deep cracks in these institutional settings, where the care was inadequate and fostered elder abuse in many forms.

We all have a role to play

The owners, managers, and our governmental bodies, who manage institutional facilities that care for our older person, have the power to address the conversation on elder abuse and to be transparent in how the care is offered to our older person. Staff, family members, visitors, volunteers, the medical community, and the older person themselves, all play a key role in ensuring that elder abuse does not rear its ugly head. Consider the following:

The Resident: The residents of institutional facilities are key players in increasing the reporting of elder abuse cases. Providing key education to residents on what elder abuse actually is, helps to increase reporting of elder abuse.

The Family: Our family members are critical in providing the love and support to their older parent, but they also serve as an extra set of eyes to ensure that their parent receives care with respect and dignity. Family members should never be afraid to advocate the best care for their loved ones. Lise Clouthier-Steel, in her book *There's No Place Like Home*, talks about her journey when her dad moved into a nursing home and the struggles that she encountered. Her book provides an excellent guide to caregivers and family. Her courage to write that book, share her experience and offer a guide to loved ones, family members and caregivers, definitely makes the book a must-read to acquire more knowledge on the subject of 'what to do' when a parent moves into a nursing home.

The Worker: Personal support workers, nurses, recreational staff, dietary staff, housekeeping and laundry staff, health workers, and administrative staff who work in institutional settings are very important and valuable staff that provide excellent care to our elderly residents. Key education and training on what elder abuse is, how to prevent it and what to do if one witnesses it, is mandatory education in our institutional facilities.

There is an increased workload on our health care staff and it is critical for the owners and managers of the institutional facilities to ensure that proper budgets are put in place, so there is an appropriate level of staffing and the workload for staff is acceptable. If the workers are not overworked, they will be less stressed, more compassionate, and able to provide the care that the older person requires and needs, free from elder abuse.

One of the heartbreaking stories to come out during the COVID-19 pandemic, was of our elderly population in institutionalized settings where some of the homes were unable to control the spread of the Coronavirus, which resulted in an increase in fatalities of our elderly residents. It becomes obvious that the level of staffing in these institutional settings is not sufficient to care for our elderly residents. The appropriate level of staffing is critical in these homes, in order to ensure that they offer a safe home environment for every resident. The personal care workers that care for the elderly are the "invisible workers" who are too often burnt-out, underpaid, understaffed, and forced to work at many different homes in order to make a decent living. This was a devastating lesson learned from COVID-19 which we must not forget.

Regulatory and Legal measures: Long-term care homes are licensed by the provincial government and in order for a resident to move in, they must meet the eligibility requirements. All long-term care homes have procedures in place that require the home to identify, assess and respond to any issues that relate to the resident. Long-term care homes have mandatory reporting for elder abuse in place. In Ontario[5] "Anyone (except another resident) who suspects someone living in a long-term care home is being abused or neglected must report it to the director of long-term care homes. The long-term care home must inform the abused resident's substitute decision-maker, where the resident is incapable, of any suspected abuse or neglect."

Retirement homes[6] are privately owned and operated for-profit and they are governed by the Retirement Homes Act and regulated by the Retirement Homes Regulatory Authority. They have the same mandatory obligation to report elder abuse. Having these regulations in place is a very large and important step in the right direction;

however, compliance and enforcement of these laws are just as important. One of the other key steps that our policy and legal makers can make is to ensure that as our elderly population grows, we increase our level of compliance and enforcement officers.

The Community: The community at large also has a large role to play in helping to ensure that our institutional facilities play a positive role in the community and are free from elder abuse. The "community" is a large group that includes our medical professionals, legal professionals, social workers, schools, neighbours and anyone and everyone that has a connection with an older person. It is important to understand and appreciate that as a community, we do not hold ageist views of these institutional settings, and see these facilities as an integral part of our community. We have further discussed the role that the community can play in Chapter 9.

There has actually been very little research done on elder abuse in institutional settings. Those studies that have been conducted show that elder abuse in these settings is very prevalent.[7] The *Elder Abuse Prevalence in Community Settings* report, states that 15.7% or approximately one in six older adults are victims of abuse.[8] This is shockingly high and elder abuse within these institutional settings is going to be a growing concern and become an even greater problem as our population ages and requires care.

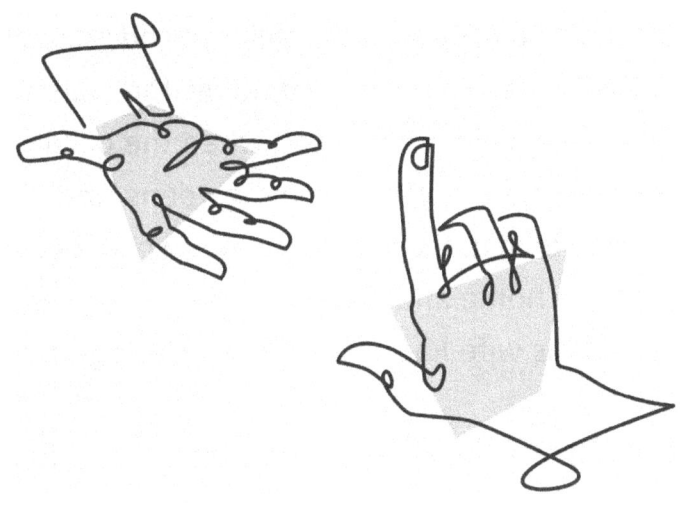

Chapter 7: Aging At Home

Many seniors will declare that they want to stay in their own homes for as long as they can and will do so by bringing in additional support for assistance with personal health care needs and the maintenance of their homes. It is expected that our older population will represent 25% of the whole population by 2031. The home care industry will have to grow to meet the needs of those who wish to stay at home.

The Story of Tracy and her Dad

Tracy was a teacher with twin girls and a loving husband. Tracy had a younger and an older brother and was a devoted daughter to her father, Thomas, who lived in the family home on his own after her mother had passed away.

Thomas loved having all of his children and grandchildren visit. He never gave up on continuing the Sunday roast tradition that his wife had started when the children were small. He enjoyed maintaining his gardens and the train station he had built in the recreation room in the basement. He enjoyed his home and sharing stories of the early days when he and his wife had started their life together in this home.

Tracy thought from time to time that her father might find it easier in a retirement home, but Thomas politely told her that they would have to carry him out in a pine box.

As the years passed, Thomas found it more and more difficult to maintain the house and the garden. Ever respectful of her father, Tracy continued to raise the possibility of moving to a retirement home, but the answer was always the same. So Tracy and her brothers hired a housekeeper and a gardener to assist once a week.

As more time passed, Thomas's health deteriorated and he began to use a walker for balance. He also needed help to get out of bed and perform his morning care, but he continued to refuse to move from his home.

Tracy and her brothers held the Power of Attorney for Personal Care and Property. He was clearly still capable of managing his property and most of his personal care. The children sat with their father and reviewed with him the things that he could do and the things that he required assistance with. It was clear to Thomas, that he needed some help with his personal care, so he agreed to a plan for personal care, which respected his desire to remain in his home. Thomas told his children that he had been doing some reading and he knew that a power of attorney for personal care should be respected and only provide for the help that he actually needed.

Tracy interviewed prospective home care agencies for their father and after a detailed interview process, a decision was made. The chosen home care agency put together a very detailed and comprehensive care plan which was closely followed by his caregiver, Mary, who followed the plan and provided Thomas with excellent care. Tracy could see that her father was happy, doing well physically and mentally and was enjoying being in his own home. Tracy used her weekends to visit with Thomas and was pleased that the care plan was working.

Sadly, Mary retired after 18 months to look after her own parents. The Home Care Agency provided another personal care worker. The new personal care worker never arrived on time and never seemed to know what care services Thomas needed, even though there was a detailed care plan that had been successfully used by Mary. Arguments with the company were not helpful because the home care agency simply sided with the care provider who attested that the care was provided even though, truthfully, they had not been there. New workers were provided, but they were not capable of implementing the care that Thomas needed. This was due to a lack of professional training and a lack of understanding of the care plan. In some cases, the care was provided in a manner that left Thomas feeling very angry and frustrated.

Tracy's contact with the home care supervisor was like a roller coaster — things would get better and then they would not. Thomas was declining both mentally and physically, so Tracy convened a family meeting with her brothers and her father. All options were reviewed, and Thomas agreed that the present plan was not working. He was ready to go to an assisted living floor of a retirement home that he had seen and approved.

The Epilogue

The abuse in this situation was the failure to provide home care as agreed. Thomas's family followed all the necessary steps by being actively involved and most importantly by keeping in touch with Thomas about his care and how it was delivered by the home care agency. Services offered by home care agencies are an important and necessary part of senior care.

The care provided by home care agencies can be very positive, and we saw how Thomas was very happy when Mary supported and cared for him. Mary was there on her mornings, she was dependable, she knew what the care plan was, and she had created a positive environment for Thomas to live life to its best. However, we also saw in this story that this is not always the case. We saw how Thomas's health deteriorated due to poor care. Thomas wanted to age in his own home. To do this, requires putting measures in place to ensure that our seniors can make the choices that they want and receive the care that they need, so that they can be independent, participate in life, and be free from abuse.

We discussed institutionalized elder abuse in the last chapter, and we believe that it is important to include and think about the care provided through home care agencies with the same sharp eye. We need to be diligent because, in many cases, the older person and the care provider are alone together most of the time. Seniors suffer neglect at the hands of home care agencies who have been found to simply not perform the care they were paid to provide. Many never turn up, or turn up at unscheduled times, leaving the older person at the mercy of the care provider. Home care providers are not supervised and there is a very big gap that we need to pay attention to and address if we do not want to see elder abuse on the rise.

It is crucial for there to be some form of oversight and procedures for accountability for the home care worker and the protection of our seniors. Home care service providers should have established standards of training and rules and regulations for their home care workers to follow.

We have seen that, even in cases like Thomas's situation, Thomas could afford the care but competent, well-trained workers who are willing to work at minimum wage, are few and far between. Thomas wanted this care and had the resources, but the home care company failed him.

Maybe some form of government supplement is required for home care workers, as an inducement to do the work that so many people will not do? Maybe we can turn to the family members to perform the personal care, by providing them with the professional training and some financial support? However, this may not be possible or even useful, until the power of attorney for property and personal care are held by different people and regulatory measures are in place for those who provide home care, be it a home care agency, caregivers, or family members.

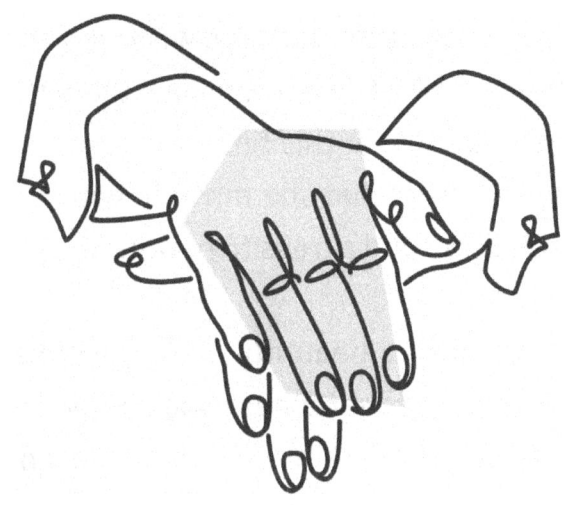

Chapter 8: Elder Abuse and Culture

Elder abuse can never happen to me! What is elder abuse? That does not happen in our culture! This is not a matter that we talk about or discuss. Many are surprised to be asked such questions. What is even more surprising and alarming is that most seniors in the ethnocultural community do not see their treatment as elder abuse. The key question to ask is how and why is this possible? What can we do about it moving forward?

The Story of Fatima

Fatima is a 75-year South-Asian woman who is very healthy and independent, but has recently lost her husband and is now required to live with her sons. She really does not want to live with her sons, but they have told her that she cannot live by herself because no one is there to look after her. Plus, it was their father's wish that the boys look after their mother. She tries to convince them that she does not need their support at this time; however, they will not listen to her and insist that she move in with them. Fatima accepts the decision and agrees to honour the wishes of her late husband.

One evening, after a beautiful dinner, Fatima overhears her four sons arguing over where she should live. The two younger sons say that mom cannot come and live with them because they are too busy with work, which entails a lot of travel. Another son says that she cannot live with him because his partner is not in agreement. The oldest son says that it is unfair that he has to have mom with him because he always has to take responsibility and his wife is not happy with this arrangement. Fatima is surprised to hear such an exchange and feels hurt that she has had this impact on them. She decides to take another opportunity and tells her children that she is happy staying where she is. But they unanimously say "no, she must stay with family and not be alone." Fatima is confused but happily agrees with the children and moves in with her older son.

The move does not go as well as Fatima had hoped. Her son starts to distance himself from her. He refers to his mother as if she has no opinion and disrespects her by calling her names and tells her that it is so unfair that he has to have responsibility for her. Fatima has no desire to ignite these feelings in her son or have any negative impact on him. Her mere presence seems to stress her older son and his wife. She is even finding that her grandchildren, who are only 8 and 9, are not playing with her as they used to. Fatima decides that it is better for her to stay in her room. Staying in her own room is lonely and it is even more hurtful when she can hear her son and family laughing and having fun. Fatima cannot understand why she is not being included in family activities. She has also found that her other sons visit less frequently with her, even though they are at her older son's house regularly. She finds that they do not listen to her concerns and always seem to unite with her older son and his views and opinions. She is surprised that they never ask her how she is doing, but instead always ask about her well-being from her older son.

As time goes by, Fatima is keeping herself more and more in her own room. She is feeling isolated and greatly misses her home, her independence, and her friends. It is now beginning to really hurt, but when she thinks about it, she reminds herself of the importance and value of family. In her culture, her parents always taught her not to look after her own individual concerns, but to think of the family and what is in the best interest of the family. She cannot go against that. However, what she cannot understand is that she had taught her children the importance of respecting elders in the family and she cannot understand why they are treating her so poorly by not showing her the love and respect that an older person should receive. Fatima feels that there is nothing that she can do. She is living with her son and is dependent on him. She has little contact with her friends and has no one to really talk to about this. She just has to endure the pain and put on a big smile. The family is really important.

The Epilogue

In discussing Fatima's case, it is important to be aware and acknowledge that when looking at an older person from the ethnocultural community, we need to look at it through the lens of their culture, their ethnicity, their life experiences, their own community, their language abilities and their status in Canada. Once we do all that, it will deepen the understanding of the concerns and issues of the older person.

Our Canadian population is ageing, and according to Statistics Canada, seniors are expected to comprise approximately 23- 25% of the population by 2036. In Canada, our senior population is more ethnoculturally diverse due to Canadian immigration policies, as well as the trends and the growth of our minority population.[9] Approximately one in five Canadians are members of the visible minority group. In order for us to address and increase awareness of elder abuse, we must look at elder abuse through the eyes of the elders that have different cultural influences.

To a neighbour looking in at Fatima, they would see an elderly mother living at home with her son. A member of the western culture would be in true admiration of Fatima since her family looks happy, content, and fortunate that different generations are able to live under the same roof. The story of Fatima is an example of silent elder abuse. There are no physical signs of abuse, no drastic financial abuse, and nothing that would send an observer or a neighbour to ask questions of how Fatima is being treated. But Fatima is a victim of elder abuse. To be able to help and support our seniors of the ethnocultural community and fight elder abuse, we need to talk about elder issues and remove the ageist views that families, communities, and society have of older people from different ethnocultural communities.

To a member of the cultural community looking on, they have the interest of wanting to protect their community. They do not want to advertise that elder abuse happens in their community. The community understands their own culture and they are in a position to help and offer support. The community as a whole, should not be afraid to talk about elder abuse and should offer tools and resources to older members of their community.

To the younger generation of the cultural community. You may have immigrated with your parents, aunts, or uncles to Canada, or you may be the first generation born in Canada. Like any other younger generation, you will see things differently from your parents' generation. This is natural and we have no objection to this; however, we would ask that you take the time to look at your parent's situation through their eyes. They are older and they have needs but it is also important to take into account your culture as well. Respect and understanding of your culture will empower you to support your elders and will play a large part in addressing elder abuse.

To the older person of a different culture, we also require you to empower yourself and understand that you also have a responsibility to speak up against elder abuse. There are people and organizations that are willing to help. We realize that this is a very difficult step to take. Reach out to members of your community, to a friend. Most importantly you need to empower yourself and know that living with elder abuse is not the only option.

At this time, there has been very little research and reporting on issues relating to elder abuse in ethnocultural communities both in Canada and worldwide. The limited research that has been conducted has been very insightful. [10] The research confirms that elder abuse has no barriers to race and culture. Elder abuse is present and exists in all societies.

Seniors of different cultural communities are very reluctant to move into a nursing or retirement home. Most cannot afford it and are either living alone or living with a family member in their home. The majority of the abuse happens in the home setting and the abuser is usually a family member or a paid caregiver, which is another reason why this abuse is typically hidden and under-reported. Members of the ethnocultural community are reluctant to report their treatment as elder abuse to the authorities or to someone that can help. There are many reasons for this, such as shame, fear, duty, and the impact that it would have on the family, and what their community would think. There are also many factors that cause and maintain elder abuse in the ethnocultural community, such as dependency on the family member, the inability to speak English or French, and a lack of friends and community support.

How Do We Move Forward?

In order for there to be a strong movement towards addressing elder abuse, it is important to focus on the key factors that allow elder abuse to grow in different cultures. Once we have a better understanding of those, we can put the next steps in place to help bring greater awareness to elder abuse. We can empower our older person to stand up against the abuse so that their life is enhanced without disrespecting their culture, traditions, and beliefs.

It starts with an older person. We must encourage them to have the ability to speak up and advocate for their own quality of life; however, this is not always possible for the following reasons. In ethnocultural communities, the importance of the family is paramount. The older person's identity is linked to the family. This has great benefits because the family is a place of comfort, warmth, and love. It is a place where the family unit cheers you on during difficult times and celebrates with you during the good. The level of mutual dependency and support that is provided in a family is very beneficial; however, what if this mutual dependency cultivates a negative environment that promotes elder abuse?

In Canada, our present immigration policies allow children to sponsor their parents to live with them, further promoting dependency.[11] We have seen cases where parents or grandparents are sponsored to come to Canada and then they spend their days looking after their grandchildren, cleaning the house, and cooking. In the ethnocultural community, the argument can be made that there is nothing wrong with this — it cultivates the family and working together is important. However, the situation changes when the child creates a high expectation and expects the work to be done, isolating the parent from the community, and controlling the parents' every movement.

Social isolation among older persons from different cultural communities is very common. The main reasons for this isolation can be the inability to speak English or French, lack of friends/peer support, and the strong dependency on family. In some cases, the abuser may take advantage of the older person by enhancing further social isolation through the restriction of social contact and limiting or misrepresenting information. This level of control perpetuates elder abuse. The older person is very reluctant and fearful to complain. Social isolation leads to mental and physical health deterioration, deterioration of social skills and, ultimately, to elder abuse.[12] Our governmental bodies at all levels have put programs in place to promote social inclusion; however, these programs need to recognize the cultural and dependency factors.

Many families that immigrate to Canada have quite a burden to carry once they land in Canada. They need to find work, establish their careers, and look after their young family. The obligation and duty to look after your parent is a strong one. Being a caregiver for your children and your parents can be very overwhelming and extremely stressful. Caregiver burn-out is a large concern in ethnocultural families. There is a strong expectation for the able child to look after their young family, as well as their elderly parents. Furthermore, for financial reasons they are unable to access additional financial support. The financial and family pressure placed on the able child leads to a higher caregiver burn-out, which causes health concerns for the caregiver. The indirect result of caregiver burden creates an environment for elder abuse. Having a good understanding of this cycle of care in ethnocultural families is important in understanding how elder abuse can occur and to provide the necessary resources. These external circumstances can be addressed by taking the time to acknowledge them and to put in place measures that help support families and hence alleviate the potential of elder abuse.

Today we are seeing great changes with equality for women inside and outside of the home. However, this was not always the case for women of every culture that are now older. Remember, these older women were subjected to a highly patriarchal society when they were younger. They may have been subjected to abuse throughout their life and they have aged with this. Abuse is all that they know and understand, and they see this as normal. The father may no longer have the strength for physical abuse and may now have changed to verbal, emotional, and psychological abuse. Their children grew up with abuse in the family environment and would continue the cycle of abuse that the father inflicted on the mother. When we turn to look at an older woman who is now subjected to elder abuse, it may be very difficult to ask her to stand up against it or to seek help. She never did so in the past, so why would she do so now? Being mindful of this is important.

The good news is that we have made great strides against domestic abuse and our younger women in ethnocultural communities will not grow older seeing abuse as normal and will stand up against it. It is important to note that some cases have arisen, where women were subjected to abuse by their partner and they are now, in fact, the abuser.

The Story of Mrs. Aaman

Take the story of Mrs. Aaman who is 85 and lives with her husband, who is 90. She had been subjected to physical, verbal, and emotional abuse all her life, but her husband is now very frail and relies on her for his care needs. Mrs. Aaman provides him with the care needed, but is verbally and emotionally abusive towards her husband. She continues the abuse that she suffered and imparts it to her husband. In a situation like this, the abuse cycle continues because this is all she knows; however, by addressing and talking about elder abuse, we can break the cycle of abuse and provide Mrs. Aaman and her husband the support that they both need.

Living in Canada is different from living in your own home country. The weather, the food, the medical system, the education system, and the westernized approach to providing care may differ from those in other nations. Many children of an older person may be unfamiliar as to how to look after their parent within their new environment. They themselves may not have the knowledge of how to care; they may not know how to cook the food that their parents enjoy, they may feel embarrassed when their parents are in need of care, and various other variables that affect their parents' day-to-day lifestyle. This lack of understanding on the part of the family member to provide the care, may be seen as a form of neglect on the part of the parent, since the child is not able to provide the care that the parent needs. It is important to reach out for help and for the community of professionals to ask questions and be aware of situations that require attention.

Elder abuse is a problem that exists all over the world and is not limited to western society.[13] This is a social and global problem. It starts with education on accepting and acknowledging that elder abuse does happen regardless of your culture.

Chapter 9: The Community - Who Can I Trust?

A Story of Acknowledgment

Lisa lived by herself in a rural community. She enjoyed her home, the community, and the small group of friends that she had. She and her husband, Bert, had raised their five children in this home and now it was just her alone. All of her children were settled in large cities, had great careers and a happy family home. Lisa's neighbour, a young single man in his 50s, was very helpful and would come around and help Lisa whenever she wanted. Lisa enjoyed the company since it was awfully lonely being alone. Lisa and the neighbour enjoyed evenings of conversation, card games and now and again a glass of red wine. Lisa was happy with their friendship and had started to put great trust in this relationship, but she started to feel very uncomfortable. He would constantly remind her that her driving was very weak and that he should drive her to all her appointments. He even started to do all her groceries, and he never bought the food that she wanted, it was always what he thought she should eat. However, Lisa agreed to what her neighbour said. He even accompanied Lisa to the bank, and he was privy to all her banking and financial affairs. Lisa knew that she was not in the right situation, but she just did not know how to reach out and get the help that she knew she needed. Who does she reach out to for help?

The Epilogue

When you are aware that you are a victim of elder abuse, or the potential of becoming a victim of elder abuse it is important to know that there are many people out there to help you. There is a community of people. You are not on your own.

One of the issues with elder abuse is that it is a hidden problem. As our population gets older, the concern surrounding our older person will become a larger discussion; however, today matters relating to elder abuse are often ignored. The main purpose of this book is to raise the issue of elder abuse and to increase the comfort level so that talking about elder abuse is acceptable, and to know that the community that we live in participates in the conversation and provides the help that is very much needed.

To increase the reporting of elder abuse we must look at the professionals that surround and service the older person. This includes the accountant, the financial planner, the banker, the lawyer, and the physician. Education on ageism and elder abuse is critical for these professionals since they have access to talk to the older person, to see visible signs of elder abuse and most importantly, the older person has already established trust with these individuals.

As a result, when these professionals are aware of the abuse, they must be empowered with the tools to increase reporting of the abuse to the police, social agencies and other family members who can help.

Family Physicians

In Lisa's case, one person that she can turn to would be her family physician. The physician is fully aware of the older person and their medical history and would be the first one to notice any physical abuse or neglect during a regular medical exam. A simple urine test will reveal a lot about a person's nutritional health. However, Dr. Mark Yaffe identified in his paper *Understanding Elder Abuse in Family Practice*,[14] that the family physicians reported the lowest number of cases of elder abuse amongst health and social workers, despite the fact that family physicians see their older patients on average 4 or 5 times per year. This may be for many reasons since the family physician wants to protect the trust of the patient and not dig too deeply into matters outside of the health matter that the older person has come to see the doctor about. You may have a victim that is reluctant to ask for help and is more willing to spend the energy denying that they are a victim of abuse.

Dr. Yaffe, Dr. Wolfson, Dr. Lithwick, and Dr. Weiss developed and created a tool that would help family physicians detect elder abuse. The tool that they created protects the trust between the family physician and the older patient, but allows the family physician to ask more questions where he/she is suspicious of elder abuse. The tool is called *The Elder Abuse Suspicion Index (EASI)*. This tool is much more effective than mandatory screening of all older patients for elder abuse. Mandatory screening leads to creating an environment where we desensitize elder abuse since many older people will know how to answer questions in a way that they are able to further disguise elder abuse. Furthermore, with mandatory screening we are encouraging ageism because we are labelling every older person as one that is a victim. The family physician can employ *The Elder Abuse Suspicion Index (EASI)* in cases where there is suspicion. *The Elder Abuse Suspicion Index (EASI)*[15] is as follows:

EASI Questions Q.1-Q.5 asked of the patient; Q.6 answered by doctor Within the last 12 months:			
1) Have you relied on people for any of the following: bathing, dressing, shopping, banking, or meals?	YES	NO	Did Not Answer
2) Has anyone prevented you from getting food, clothes, medication, glasses, hearing aids or medical care, or from being with people you wanted to be with?	YES	NO	Did Not Answer
3) Have you been upset because someone talked to you in a way that made you feel shamed or threatened?	YES	NO	Did Not Answer
4) Has anyone tried to force you to sign papers or to use your money against your will?	YES	NO	Did Not Answer
5) Has anyone made you afraid, touched you in ways that you did not want, or hurt you physically?	YES	NO	Did Not Answer
6) Doctor: Elder abuse may be associated with findings such as poor eye contact, withdrawn nature, malnourishment, hygiene issues, cuts, bruises, inappropriate clothing, or medication compliance issues. Did you notice any of these today or in the last 12 months?	YES	NO	Unsure

The Elder Abuse Suspicion Index (EASI)[16] has been a very successful tool; a review of the tool has shown that it only takes 2 minutes to ask, and 97.2% of doctors felt it would have a moderate to a big impact on their practice. As we educate our family physicians on elder abuse and increase the awareness of this matter, we will see an increase in reporting and detection of elder abuse.

It is also important to recognize that increasing the education and providing tools to our family physicians for the detection of elder abuse will have an indirect impact on educating other medical professionals that are connected to providing care to our older person, such as our nurses, physiotherapists, chiropractors, mental health care providers, and other medical professionals.

Family physicians can also provide care to their elderly patients by virtual means. One example of such a digital tool is called eConsult. These virtual tools are highly effective, in that they allow the medical professionals to collaborate with other medical professionals at the same time and provide access to medical care to our senior population in the comfort of their own home. These digital tools can be a great benefit in helping the fight against elder abuse for many reasons, such as:

1. It takes away the stress of the older person having to travel and struggle to get to their medical appointment, especially if there are physical concerns with walking.

2. It reduces dependency on another person to drive the older person to a medical appointment.

3. It provides more time for the doctor to ask questions and collaborate with other medical professionals on the call.

4. When an appointment is provided in the comfort of your own home, even though it is virtual, you are allowing the doctor to come into your "home," which creates a level of comfort and security to benefit the older person.

With respect to institutional care in a nursing home and in retirement homes, the family physician is a valuable resource that can help promote a higher degree of care and support for our older person. The family physician can increase the accountability of these institutions in the care that they provide to the older person, which is something that we greatly need. The role that our medical professionals can and do play in combatting elder abuse is key.

Financial and Investment Advisors

In our story, Lisa's neighbour accompanied her to the bank and was privy to all her banking affairs. In Lisa's situation, the bank representatives did not think anything of it or ask any questions that would provide the protection and safety that Lisa needed. We need the support of our bank tellers, and financial and investment advisors, to be aware of elder abuse, and be educated on what elder abuse is and how it rears its ugly head in the financial world. Increased knowledge and discussion around elder abuse will increase reporting and enhance the tools to fight elder abuse. It will also increase the trust relationship that our older person has with their financial and investment advisors and provide a great vehicle for our financial and investment advisors to play a role in protecting our older person from financial abuse and therefore increase the reporting of elder abuse. The Canadian Foundation for the Advancement of Investor Rights has recognized how urgent the protection of our older person is from financial abuse and raised a strong awareness of elder abuse in the investment and financial industry[17]. It is also important for the financial and investment advisors to turn to the older person and ask questions to them. You will be surprised how savvy an older person is with respect to financial matters.

Family and Caregivers

Lisa has a family of five children and turning to them for support is important. Families are the ones that we trust and who we turn to in times of difficulty and need. As we get older, the support and love of our families becomes even more essential, especially when there are care needs involved. In most cases, the care from our families is provided with love and compassion. It is important to recognize that there are times when caring for an older family member can be stressful. There is no doubt that the emotional and physical demands of caregiving can take a toll on the caregiver. Research has shown that caregiver stress is one of the causes of elder abuse.[18] To address elder abuse in these situations, it is important to look at support for the families that take on the role of a caregiver.

Educating the family caregiver and letting them know that they are not alone, and to reach out for help is important. Support from other family members, friends and community is acceptable.

Important conversations with the caregiver and the older person should be encouraged. There are times when the family caregiver cannot see the stress that is mounting upon them, but the older parent can. These conversations are critical to ensure that the important relationship between the family members is maintained and that the seed of elder abuse is not planted. You will be surprised how open and understanding the older person is. Working together and collaborating will provide a solution that will meet the needs of the older person, the caregiver, and the family unit as a whole. This is a legacy that the older person wants to nurture and all that is required is a conversation.

Caregivers need to be leaders in their own care, as well as the care of the older person. Accessing care and support for the caregiver is important for their mental health. We encourage the caregiver to remember that you cannot look after a loved one unless you look after yourself. If you are tired or exhausted, then the person who will feel that most will be the person who you are providing the care to. Caregivers must advocate for caregiving as well.

Where the past relationship with the family caregiver and the older person has not been strong, then the family should ask the question as to whether this person should be the primary caregiver of the loved one. It is important to foster a positive relationship with the older person, rather than to stress it with day-to-day care. In Canada, we have nursing homes, retirement homes and private-home daycare services, that are available to provide the care that the older person requires without compromising the foundation of the loving family relationship, which may crumble into the pits of elder abuse. With respect to institutional care, the family must play their role and visit their loved one and work with the institutional facility to ensure their loved one is receiving the best care.

Key Community Members

In Canada, we are very fortunate to have excellent social agencies, community centres, social workers, health care providers, the police, and our front-line workers that support and assist our older person each and every day—be it with their groceries, driving them to appointments, or volunteering their time. It takes a community to support and empower the vulnerable members of society. The community plays a critical role in helping to protect the older person against elder abuse. The more eyes and ears that are trained to watch for the signs of elder abuse, the more the community as a whole, can do to keep the abuser at bay. The more that we, as a community, openly discuss elder abuse and acknowledge its existence, then the more we will be in a position of strength to support the older person and create a society that will have no tolerance for elder abuse.

Chapter 10: You Must Use Your Voice

The Story of Mrs. Mahar

Mrs. Mahar has enjoyed living on her own for over twenty years. After her husband passed away and her three daughters moved out of the family home, Mrs. Mahar decided to move into a small apartment. She enjoyed the new friends that she had made in the building, and the social evening on Friday nights was always something to look forward to. Her daughters did not live far away from the apartment and she had an open invitation to their home, which Mrs. Mahar took full advantage of.

In the last year, Mrs. Mahar's physical movement became greatly limited and she was unable to move around unless she had a walker. She did not feel comfortable visiting her children at their home anymore because of the steps. The children, of course, made every effort to make their mom feel comfortable but Mrs. Mahar refused to visit. Mrs. Mahar also stopped attending activity classes and socializing with her friends in the apartment. Over time she became more and more alone.

The lack of socialization with her friends and family directly impacted Mrs. Mahar's mental and physical health. Mrs. Mahar had one nephew, whom she had not heard from in quite a while, and he began to visit her on a regular basis at her home. The relationship with her nephew grew stronger. She trusted her nephew; however, her nephew had other plans. He took advantage of the position that Mrs. Mahar was in and endorsed her to stay at home alone. He did everything for Mrs. Mahar, including the grocery shopping and her banking. Over time, he quietly helped himself to Mrs. Mahar's long-term savings. He then disappeared leaving Mrs. Mahar without her savings and the friendship that she thought she had nurtured.

The Epilogue

What happened to Mrs. Mahar is very unfortunate. It is important to plan for old age before you get there. Take the time to understand and prepare for what elder abuse is and what it looks like. Never work with the mindset that it can 'never happen to me'. Recognition that elder abuse is happening to you or someone else is a key element in combatting it at an early stage. You are right, it will never happen to you, if you know how to prepare for it. If you do not, then like Mrs. Mahar, you will end up giving away important financial information. You can plan and prevent these events by making sure that you have your financial affairs in order and that a power of attorney for property and personal care is carefully prepared.

Mrs. Mahar had a good social group in her apartment building. She had a great relationship with her daughters. Yes, Mrs. Mahar's physical condition had changed, and she had to use a wheelchair. But please do not let changes in your life stop you from talking about how you feel. Older persons should share and talk more freely about their situation with their loved ones. Once you reach out for support, then you have the right people in place to help guard you against those that can take advantage of you.

Social isolation of the older person is critical to an abuser's chances of success. Mrs. Mahar distanced herself from her family and her friends and by so doing, she allowed her nephew to take advantage of her.

Your social relationships are important to you.[19] They are even more important when you are an older person. A study conducted by Harvard University[20] on what constitutes happiness is a strong voice that specifies that happiness is not based on what wealth or status you carry, but on the quality of your social relationships. The study showed that looking at a person's quality of social relationships will provide strong indicators of how well they age. As we age, our social relationships become more and more important to us. Those who have very little social connection and are isolated, are at greater risk of elder abuse.

Technology plays a key role in promoting social health. Mrs. Mahar did not want to go and visit her children because of the difficulty of using the steps. However, social health can still be promoted via technology. Families can connect and stay connected through social media, facetime, and video calls. We must acknowledge and embrace technology, as well as the benefit that it can bring for enhancing our social health. The biggest concern with technology is the potential for abuse to occur, especially for an older person. Many see technology as a ground for breeding elder abuse. However, this does not have to be the case. Any situation can be grounds for breeding elder abuse. We cannot deny the benefit of making friends through technology because of the fear of potential elder abuse. Instead, we must acknowledge this fear, and use courage to deal with it. When we talk more and more about elder abuse, about ageism and about the importance of being an older person, then we are able to see the signs of what elder abuse is.

As we are writing this section of the book, the majority of the globe is in quarantine due to COVID-19, with the politicians and the health care providers educating the world on the importance of physical distancing. We as human beings need to socialize and we are social creatures; however, what COVID-19 has taught us is the "silver lining" that we can still socialize and obtain the emotional and physiological support through technology. What has provided us with hope are the stories that we hear of the younger generation teaching the older generation on how to connect with them through technology. The older generations have taken to this technology to connect with their friends, family and loved ones. This is a great example of the world working together and putting aside preconceived views and opinions of the older person and being more socially connected.

Mrs. Mahar has a responsibility to look after her own health and to reach out for support when she needs it. Taking time to look after your physical and mental health is important. This involves making sure that you follow a healthy diet, exercise, and maintain a good sleep routine. Your mental and emotional health is just as important as your physical health. The consequences of not looking after your mental and emotional health will put you at risk for elder abuse. It is much easier to take advantage of an older person who has low self-esteem and low self-confidence. The support of family members, as well as social, mental and health professionals, is vitally important and should be accessed to provide you with the support that you need.

Please remember that elder abuse does not work if someone other than the abuser is available to the elder person to communicate and associate with on a regular basis. We saw that with Mrs. Mahar and how her nephew, with whom she had little contact, had entered into her life. Abusers are like vampires – they need to be alone to hurt their victims. Abusers never seek the light of day; they seek to hide the activities of abuse. Once exposed, they flee and leave their victims alone. This is where the older person has the responsibility to help address elder abuse.

We recognize, as we wrote this book, that it requires a whole community to address elder abuse. We found that it was difficult for both of us to write for just one reader because that is not the reality. We understand that it is the older person who is being subjected to abuse and the natural tendency is to go out and provide help. But, the other members of this community, the family, the neighbours, the medical and financial community, cannot do this without the help of you, the older person. There is a large responsibility for you to speak up and surround yourself with people that you trust and who have your best interest at heart. This puts measures in place to protect yourself from abuse. In this story, without Mrs. Mahar having a support network in place, there was no one that could have helped her against her nephew.

In our view, the key to reducing the damage caused by elder abuse is early recognition of the problem as it occurs and early intervention before any significant damage occurs. This is where we, the writers, are talking to you the older person. We strongly believe that the role that you can play in addressing elder abuse is an important one. You have a voice. You must use that voice. There is a responsibility that does fall upon you. Please don't be afraid to exercise this responsibility.

Chapter 11: What Makes Us Think The Way We Do?

The recognition of elder abuse as a social problem is just being understood. As our population ages, more and more are realizing that this is a problem that they face personally, or that someone very close in their community is facing. It is only when we talk about elder abuse and are comfortable about this subject that we will see an increase in reporting.[21]

But have you ever thought about why it is that we think the way we do about elder abuse and ageing? Why is elder abuse an under-reported crime? According to Statistics Canada, approximately 7 in 10 older people will not report that they are subjected to elder abuse. They suffer this abuse in silence. Why is that and how can you change that?

Does our society not offer a safe environment for them to report it? Are our seniors not being offered the same level of respect and recognition as other members of society? The answer at this time is NO and that is because of ageism.

Ageism was first defined by Robert Butler, in his book, *Why Survive? Being Old in America* as "a process of systematic stereotyping of and discrimination against people because they are old".[22] Living in an ageist society is not healthy and is one of the main factors that promote the seed of elder abuse. Until we address ageism, the battle against elder abuse will be a difficult one. Anne-Sophie Parent[23] provided the following message: *"An ageist society is an abusive society. If we continue to think that older people are inevitably dependent, frail, precarious, and excluded, we will contribute to elder abuse, rather than address it. To end elder abuse, we first need to say no to ageism and take concrete action!"*

It is important to understand and respect that not all older people are frail, weak, or dependent. Like any other age group of the population, people experience life differently. Butler clearly stated that the older years are dependent on many factors, rather than just age. They are dependent on our mental, physical and emotional health, previous life experiences, social connections, family, social support, finances, health care, and housing. Each person will experience older years differently; however, we live in a society that greatly values youth. It is a billion-dollar industry where people spend money to look as young as possible. We have advertising slogans that promote ageism, such terms as "anti-ageing". We would never see and tolerate statements that promoted racism or gender, but with respect to age, it is different, why?

The implication of ageism is that it is seen as normal behaviour to "make jokes of the older person", to think that they know so little, to think that they have memory issues and cannot remember, or that they are not flexible to change with the times and learn new activities and technology. Researchers have shown that "ageism" is one form of prejudiced thinking that is so ingrained and seen as normal behaviour. Society does not see it as problematic like other "isms".[24] The younger members of our society are given more value and the older members of society are seen as a burden. When our society thinks like this, and it is seen as normal behaviour, then we are not providing the right environment and platform for the elder person to speak up against their treatment of elder abuse by another person. As the baby boomer generation gets older, we will see the face of the Canadian population change.[25] Our society is moving towards an older society and the views and opinions that we have of the older person will change and adapt as our demographics change.

A Change in Thinking is Required

Having a positive approach to ageing is beneficial to your health,[26] and ensures that we respect the individuality of an older person. Education on ageing and respect for the older person is critical and must start as early as possible, preferably in the school system.

For example, a mother who lives with her adult daughter and her young granddaughter is often excluded from family game night because the daughter believed that her mom was incapable of playing. The granddaughter would see this and would comment, "Grandma can come and sit with us; or Grandma can play." This innocent statement changes the dynamics for the grandmother to feel included and not isolated because of a stereotypical view that her daughter holds and which her granddaughter does not hold.

Education in the workplace, for professionals and for the older person is another key step to looking at the ageing process as positive. Embracing the older person in the workplace, in the community and in conversation, are all key factors that will help deal with elder abuse. We will see more growth in the work environment where the younger workers will listen and share the knowledge that our older workers can impart upon them. Also, when we create an environment where older worker's knowledge and experience are more readily accepted, we will see the great legacy of knowledge being shared between generations, which will benefit our society and economy. Promoting a society that is more intergenerational, where the younger and the older members of society interact, will further enhance acceptance and respect for each generation.

Our legal, government, and policy members also have a role to play in promoting change and creating positive environments where elder abuse is talked about and addressed. Canada has legislated to prohibit discrimination based on age under the *Canadian Charter of Rights and Freedoms*, as well as under the *Canadian Human Rights Act*. In 2007, the Federal Government established the National Seniors Council to advise the government on key issues affecting seniors; here in Ontario, we have seen mandatory legal reporting imposed upon workers in retirement homes and long-term care to report elder abuse. There is still so much more that needs to be done and can be done.

Accepting the Ageing Process

We do understand that accepting the ageing process is not easy for many people. Elaine Smookler, a registered psychotherapist, discusses the importance of embracing the ageing process in her article *"Anti-Aging? No Thanks."* She discusses how we need to embrace our impermanence. It is this acceptance that then helps us to "enjoy the changes of life, the new discoveries that come with every ageing breath." Living in fear of ageing is not the right path. David Corbett, in his book Portfolio Life, said that "Ageing is becoming less a chronological state and more a state of mind." We need to promote the emotional and psychological health of our mature residents.

Our policymakers have a large role that they can help play in combatting ageism. Sarah Raposo and Laura Carstensen[27] summarized it as follows: *"The presence of substantial numbers of older people offers societies a resource that has never before existed—millions of experienced, wise, older citizens who are healthier and better educated than any previous generation. To allow all individuals the opportunities to age successfully, it is crucial to combat ageism in workplace structures and policies, beliefs about ageing that discourage interventions, and research practices that conflate normal ageing with disease states. We must not aim too low. By addressing these issues, we can revise knowledge about ageing and begin to redesign the life course to reap the individual and societal benefits that longer lives represent."*

Unlike other "isms" that our society has been subjected to, "ageism" is one "ism" that we will all be subjected to as we get older. This is a matter that impacts all of us and as a society, we should all work together to address the great value that being an older person offers. When an older person is truly valued, this will have a positive impact on reducing the incidences of elder abuse in our society.

Ageism is a global challenge. We encourage everyone to read the Global report on ageism developed by the World Health Organization and the UN which is available online at www.who.int. Ageism impacts everyone and we can all make a difference.

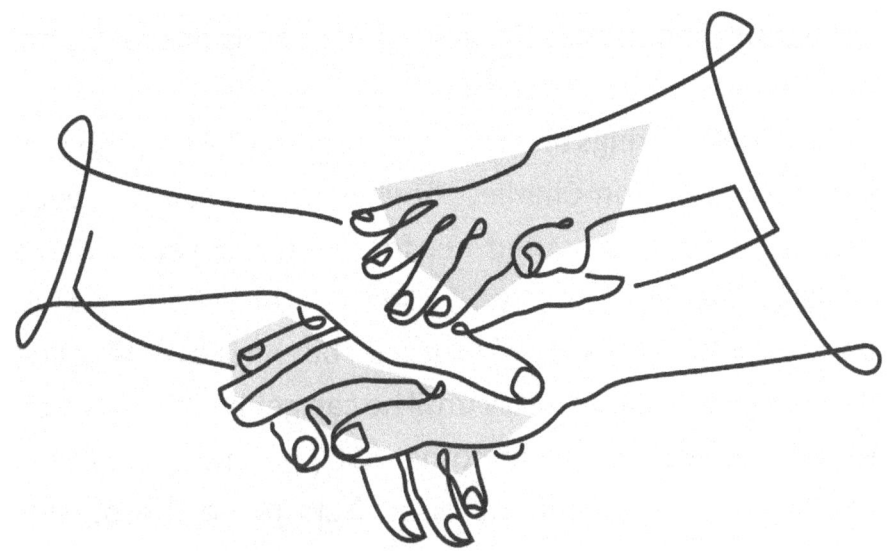

Chapter 12: We All Have a Role to Play

In *As You Like It*, Shakespeare wrote that "All the world's a stage and all the men and women merely players. They have their exits and their entrances and each man in his time plays many parts."

Imagine you are a member of a theatre audience. You are the neighbour and friend of Mrs. Jones. As the play opens, Mrs. Jones is by herself on the stage. Mrs. Jones is 75 years old. She lives by herself. She has been a widow for several years and has managed to keep her house in order. She can drive a car, but does not like to drive. Her front yard could use a little work, but she can't start the lawnmower. She gets by on her husband's survivor pension of about $50,000 per annum and her regular government pensions for a total of around $75,000 per annum.

The doorbell rings and Mrs. Jones receives a surprise visit from her grandson Charlie. She is happy to see him even though he has not visited her for at least a year. Charlie explains that he has been kicked out of school and his parents' house because of drug use, but he is over that and is looking for a place to stay until he can get back on his feet. He offers to pay his grandmother $500 per month to live in her finished basement. He also offers to do the outside chores and drive his grandmother to her appointments and the grocery store. Charlie says he will return to school in the fall. Mrs. Jones says she needs time to think about it, as this presents a big change in her life.

Scene two opens with Charlie outside her house ringing her doorbell again. Mrs. Jones appears anxious and afraid, but she opens the door. Charlie is there, suitcase in hand, ready to move in. Mrs. Jones was going to reject his proposal, but Charlie is her daughter's child, so she acquiesces.

As the play progresses, everything is smooth until it is time for Charlie to pay the rent. Charlie explained that he was still looking for a job, but it was tough for a person in his situation. He would catch up with her next month for sure. Charlie did not have the rent money, but he did carry on and do the chores and took his grandmother to the stores. Then one day, Charlie asked his grandmother to co-sign a loan for $50,000 so he could get into a landscaping business with a friend. Charlie explained it was not like she was borrowing the money because he was also signing for the loan himself and he would keep up the payments.

Mrs. Jones thought if she did this he could get out of the house and support himself. So off they went together to the bank. Mrs. Jones had never met the loan manager because she had never taken out a loan in her life and her credit rating was pristine.

Charlie talked a good story about the business and even his grandmother said he knew his way around a lawnmower. The loan manager looked up Mrs. Jones' bank history and never even asked for Charlie's ID, which would have revealed he was only 16 years old. The transaction was concluded that day and Charlie received a bank draft for $50,000 which he promptly put into a chequing account at the same branch in his own name. Over the next month, Charlie took the money out in $5,000 bundles. He paid his rent up to date with his grandmother.

In the final scene, two police investigators appear at Mrs. Jones' front door with a search warrant. They find bundles of cocaine in Charlie's closet having a street value of over a half-million dollars. Charlie is arrested and sentenced to three years in juvenile detention. Mrs. Jones has a heart attack and falls into a deep depression.

I was her friend. How did I allow this to happen? Every Thursday afternoon, we alternated visits for high tea with bran muffins. I met Charlie on one of our visits. Seemed like a nice kid. Did I ask what he was doing in the house? How long he would be staying? Why was it I had never seen him before now? Mrs. Jones said Charlie was just staying there for a while to help her out a bit.

I had been friends with Mrs. Jones for 25 years. I lived just across the street and knew her daughter, Charlie's mother, very well. I had her phone number for emergencies and she later told me about Charlie being expelled from school for selling drugs. My friend Mrs. Jones never mentioned this.

There had been no secrets between us in the past, but there had definitely been something strange about this situation. Mrs. Jones' discomfort and lack of forthrightness were unusual. The lack of details told me there was a problem. The problem was that she was not acting like my friend anymore. She had become anxious and evasive when I asked her more questions.

She told me later: "As soon as I let him move in, I knew that I had made a mistake, but it was my daughter's only son, so what could I say? He was open about his problem and his expulsion from school. Fall was just a few months away. He caught me by surprise with his request to co-sign a loan, but he seemed genuine, so I never checked with his parents."

Both Charlie and Mrs. Jones would have told me the same story about their plans if I had asked them. But I did not.

Abuse will cease when a third person joins the group. Charlie only wanted two.

If you were in my shoes, you would have asked Charlie what happened to the $50,000. He would have been angry at the question and pleaded to his grandmother for help.

But interfering would have caused him to pause. Mrs. Jones and I could have gone to my house for safety and we could have called the police. The police do not need a search warrant because Mrs. Jones can give permission for them to enter. She wanted it to end. Her reluctance came from her betrayal of her grandson. Who am I betraying by sticking my nose into my friend's business? You cannot go to jail for being nosy even if you are wrong.

I was in a position to see everything one needed to see—that both of them were trying to hide. More questions and I might have been able to bring this to an end before she lost her money.

What about some of the other players in this story? How about Charlie's parents letting him move in with his grandmother with his personal history? They did not want the shame of their failure as parents to be spotlighted for all to see.

As Mrs. Jones' good friend, I could have called Charlie's parents and asked them how they could let Charlie go to his grandmother's house to live. Maybe I could have demanded that they act like parents and reclaim their failure, leaving Mrs. Jones to her own relief. There may have been other members of her family that would have been interested in my point of view and wished to protect Mrs. Jones as well. I have seen families circle the wagons as they develop a heightened interest in their own proprietary rights in an elderly person's "estate".

There are many people out there who could fill the theatre seats. Like so many before them, they will take everything they learn about Mrs. Jones and Charlie, but may feel it would not be proper to interfere in their business. The only way that elder abuse will be stopped is if it is exposed at an early stage before very much damage can be done. You must speak up.

If you have your eyes and ears open, you will know when something is potentially not right, and you will save a lot of heartache for those victims who never report their own abuse to anyone.

About the Authors

John Johnson

Twenty-five years ago, the words "elder abuse," were not part of my vocabulary. On December 31st, 2015, after having spent 42 years in the practice of law, I made the decision to retire. My position at that time was as leader of the Estates Administration Practice Group and I was substantially involved in the litigation of estate cases.

I had been introduced to the area of elder abuse by a great number of my clients whose senior relatives were being physically and psychologically abused by other members of their own family, mainly with the object of taking their property. They systematically made the lives of these senior family members as miserable as possible. What had surprised me most about these cases was how often this was happening in families and how the same story was being told over, and over again.

A few years before I retired, I had been asked by the Council on Aging of Ottawa to join their Board of Directors and to chair their Elder Abuse Committee. The members of this committee were mostly front-line workers from across Eastern Ontario, Ottawa, and the Ottawa Valley. They were my teachers, and they were dedicated to assisting victims of elder abuse. Through a network of police officers, social workers, medical doctors, and nurses, they kept careful track of all their caseloads and saw firsthand how difficult it was looking after the needs of seniors who were harmed physically and mentally by their abusers. For these workers, the senior's safety was always paramount. This gave me the opportunity to visit the places where the front-line workers did their intake. My sadness was, and is, that most of the harm was done by the time these seniors were rescued.

For several years I have been a director of a Provincial Abuse Organization, known as ONPEA (Ontario Network for the Prevention of Elder Abuse), later known as EAO (Elder Abuse Ontario), and now known as EAPO (Elder Abuse Prevention Ontario). Until recently, I was Vice-Chair of EAPO until my term ended in late 2020.

EAPO is a charitable, not-for-profit organization dedicated to the protection of older citizens in Ontario from abuse. Their work is carried out through advocacy, education, and distribution of information via conferences, seminars, and their website. They are not front-line workers, but they do receive calls that they can refer to the appropriate assistance for the abused person. EAPO also collects statistics produced by various third parties such as the National Initiative for the Care of the Elderly, and of course, Statistics Canada. Almost all of their work is accessible through their website, which can be reached at eapon.ca, the value of which cannot be overstated.

Today I am a bona fide senior citizen over the age of 70 years, which makes me a baby boomer. It also magnifies the problem of elder abuse because there are more people who are 65 years of age than there are 15-year-olds in Canada. With the wisdom gained from my experience at EAPO, I have been blessed with an education not available elsewhere. This enabled the successful resolution of the cases I presented for abused seniors in the courts, so I feel qualified in saying that the solution lies with the early recognition of the abuse and early intervention between the abuser and the victim of the abuse.

That is what this book is about. You will see a review of all the types of abuse, including useful statistics, a roadmap to recognition at a very early stage, and early involvement with the least embarrassment to the victim of elder abuse.

While writing this book, I thought about the indigenous community and any objection they might have to the use of the word "elder" in elder abuse. It could be misconstrued with their use of the expression "elders" as it relates to their community leaders, but I do not believe they would object as what I am advocating for is that our society have respect for our "elders" and that we find a way to address the growing problem of abuse that our older members of society are falling prey to.

I also know that I still have much to learn. During the time I have taken to write this book, I have been blessed with the contribution of Sabby Duthie, a former articling student at my law firm. Sabby came forward and offered to write about the subject of cultural and institutional abuse.

Sabby Duthie

In addition to studying law, I have been the owner and operator of two retirement homes in the Ottawa and Leeds & Grenville area. I grew up in England in a southeast Asian family where respect for an older person was instilled within me and the responsibility for the care for the older person must remain within the family unit.

I have always had a strong passion for the well-being of the older person, and the firm belief that the older person has a voice that should be used and heard. I have just turned fifty years old myself and have learned valuable lessons about ageing, which my residents have shared with me during the years of working in the retirement home industry.

Working in an institutional setting for over 20 years, I was very much surprised to see how our society looked upon, and even assisted in, creating an environment for elder abuse to exist. In the operation of my retirement homes, the voice of the older person was strongly reinforced within the home; however, this is not always the case in institutional settings. We are fortunate today to have regulations in place on elder abuse in institutional settings. That said, I must admit that we still have a very long way to go in moving towards a society where elder abuse is addressed with the same vengeance as it strikes the older person being abused.

This book has clearly been a portal that opens up a great opportunity to make a difference in the older person's life. Having a conversation about elder abuse is one of the key steps to take towards addressing and providing respect to the older person.

Dedications by John Johnson

Debbie Nesbitt worked for me as a Legal Assistant for many years at Nelligan O'Brien Payne LLP. Her skill at reading my handwriting and correcting my grammar has been put to good use in the preparation of my part of the text of this book. I still know Latin, but a typing course would have been handy.

Emily Johnson is a media and communications expert in the federal government. She is also my daughter with a gift for getting the message right. Her favourite quote is, "Did you really mean to say that?"

Patricia den Boer is the editor of the magazine *Fifty-Five Plus,* where I contributed legal articles for over 15 years. Her thoughts and guidance in the preparation of this book have been of incalculable value and has kept us on the right path in presenting this important topic.

Dedications by Sabby Duthie

A special thank you goes to my special friends, Giovanna Roccamo, Naveenta Anand, Tracy Murphy and my partner, Ray Welburn. To my three daughters, Nitara, Neola, and Nerisa who were pretty much always with me on weekends and evenings in the retirement homes that we owned and operated. They have listened to my constant talk concerning issues surrounding the older person and how we can do things better. I thank them for their love, audience, patience and the support that they have provided me during the writing of this book.

I thank the staff, residents and their families of the Retirement Residences that I have run and operated over the past 20 years. The wisdom, stories, and conversations that they have shared with me have provided the strong foundation of support for this book. Each and every one of my staff, residents, and their families will always hold a special place in my heart.

Maxine Baveridge is a very dear friend of mine and a business partner. She is a keen reader and writer and is working on her own fiction book. Maxine read the book from the reader's perspective and provided valuable ideas and suggestions that have allowed us to ensure that the message of this book will be well received.

Resources & Helplines[28]

ALBERTA
Family Violence Info Line: 310-1818 toll-free
Safeguards for Vulnerable Adults Info & Reporting: 1-888-357-9339

BRITISH COLUMBIA
VictimLink BC: 1-800-563-0808
Health & Seniors Info Line: 1-800-465-4911
Seniors First BC: Seniors Abuse Info Line:
1-866-437-1940

MANITOBA
Seniors Abuse Support Line: 1-888-896-7183
Seniors Info Line: 1-800-665-6565
Protection for Persons in Care: 1-866-440-6366

NEW BRUNSWICK
Department of Social Development Adult Protection: 1-866-444-8838
Chimo Helpline: 1-800-667-5005
Seniors Information Line: 1-855-550-0552

NEWFOUNDLAND AND LABRADOR
Seniors Resource Centre: 1-800-563-5599
Royal Newfoundland Constabulary - St. John's:
709-729-8000

NORTHWEST TERRITORIES
Family Violence Crisis Line: 1-866-223-7775
Seniors Information Line: 1-800-661-0878.
Yellowknife 920-7444
Regional Health & Social Services –
Yellowknife: 867-873-7224

NOVA SCOTIA
Adult Protection/Protection for Persons in Care:
1-800-225-7225
Seniors Abuse Line: 1-877-833-3377
Seniors Info Line: 1-800-670-0065

NUNAVUT
Elders Support Line: 1-866-684-5056

ONTARIO
Seniors Safety Line: 1-866-299-1011
Long-Term Care ACTION Line: 1-866-434-0144
Retirement Home Complaints Response & Info Service: 1-855-275-7472

PRINCE EDWARD ISLAND
Seniors' Line: 1-866-770-0588
Adult Protection Services – Charlottetown:
902-368-4790
PEI Family Violence Prevention Services:
1-800-240-9894

QUEBEC
Ligne Aide Abus Aînés: 1-888-489-2287
Centre d'aide aux victimes d'actes criminels:
Québec: 1-866-532-2822 • Montréal: 514-277-9860

SASKATCHEWAN
Saskatchewan Service for Seniors: 1-306-668-2762
Seniors Information Line: 1-888-823-2211
Saskatoon Crisis Centre: 1-306-933-6200:
Prince Albert & Area: 1-306-764-1011
Regina & Area: 1-302-757-0127:
For financial abuse call: 1-306-975-8310

YUKON
Seniors' Services/Adult Protection:
1-800-661-0408 ext. 3946
Victim Services/Family Violence Prevention:
1-800-661-0408 ext. 8500
VictimLink (24 hour crisis line) - 1-800-563-0808

Resources on Elder Abuse
seniors.gc.ca

This book has served as a portal that opens up a great opportunity to make a difference in the older person's life. Having a conversation about elder abuse is one of the key steps towards addressing and providing respect to the older person.

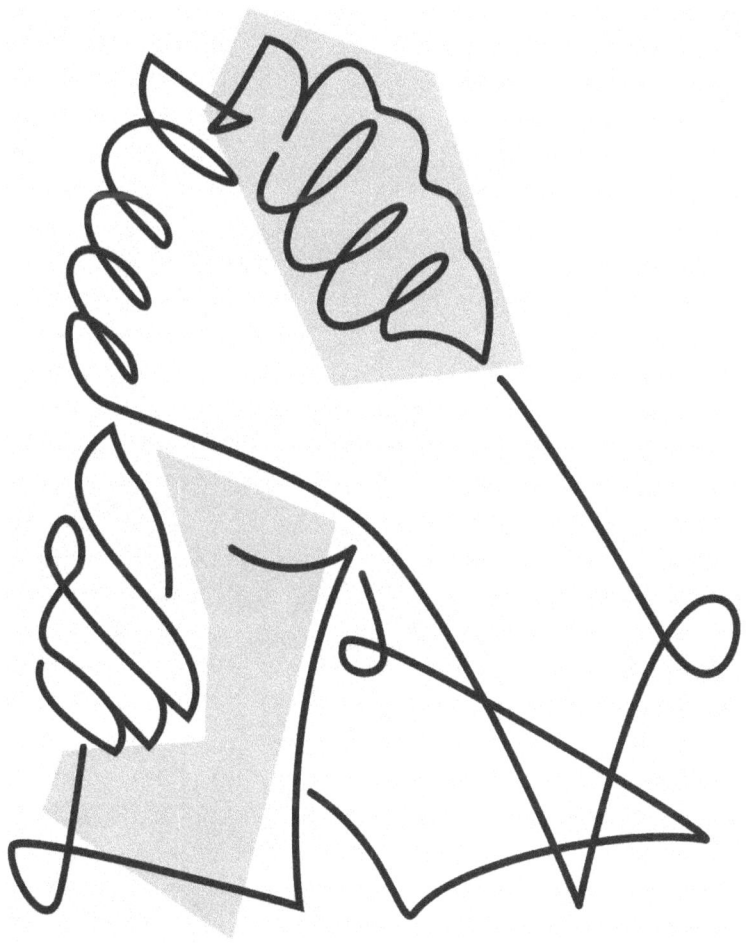

References

[1] See Canadian Family Physician, Vol. 58, December 2012

[2] Understanding Elder Abuse in Family Practice, MJ Yaffe, B. Tazkarji - Canadian Family Physician, Vol. 58, December 2012, Box 2

[3] Understanding Elder Abuse in Family Practice. MJ Yaffe, B Tazkarji. Canadian Family Physician, Vol. 58, December 2012, Box 3 – Data from National Centre on Elder Abuse

[4] World Health Organization. A Global Response to Elder Abuse and Neglect: Building Primary Health Care Capacity to Deal with the Problem Worldwide: Main Report. Geneva: WHO Press, 2008

[5] Long-Term Care Homes Act, 2007, SO 2007, c.8

[6] Retirement Homes Act, 2010, S.O. 2020, c. 11.

[7] The Prevalence of Elder Abuse in Institutional settings: a systematic review and meta-analysis. Yongie Yon, Maria Ramior-Gonzalez, Christopher R Mikton, Manfred Huber, Dinesh Sethi, European Journal of Public Health, Volume 29, Issue 1, February 2019

[8] Elder Abuse Prevalence in Community Settings: a systematic review and meta-analysis. Yon Y, Mikton CR, Gassoumis ZD, Wilber KH. Lancet Glob Heal 2017

[9] Podnieks, E. (2008). Elder abuse: The Canadian experience. Journal of Elder Abuse and Neglect, 20(2), 126-150.
DOI http://dx.doi.org/10.1080/08946560801974612

[10] Haukioja, Heather Seija Marguerite. "Exploring the Nature of Elder Abuse in Ethno-Cultural Minority Groups: A Community-based Participatory Research Study." The Arbutus Review 7, no. 1 (2016): 51. doi:10.18357/tar71201615681.

[11] Family reunification is one the great pillars of the Canadian immigration system, where a permanent resident can sponsor a parent or grandparent to live with them in Canada. The sponsor must agree to financially support their family member in the case that their relative cannot provide for their own needs. This is to ensure that the new permanent resident will not require government

assistance. The length of this financial obligation depends on the individual being sponsored:

- **Spouse, common-law, or conjugal partner:** 3 years
- **Dependent child**: 10 years OR when the child reaches age 22 (whichever comes first); 3 years for a dependent child over age 22.
- **Parent or grandparent**: 20 years

Note that this financial obligation does not disappear if the sponsored person becomes a citizen, divorces, or separates from the sponsor, or moves away from Canada. (Immigration Canada)

[12] "Social Isolation of Seniors: A Focus on New Immigrant and Refugee Seniors in Canada." CNPEA, cnpea.ca/en/tools/practice-tools/899-social-isolation-of-seniors-a-focus-on-new-immigrant-and-refugee-seniors-in-canada.

[13] At the time of writing this book in order to combat elder abuse in the ethnic community a need for more focused research is still required, "Culture Diversity and Elder Abuse: Implications for ..." Accessed June 8, 2019. https://www.researchgate.net/publication/286978899_Culture_ diversity and elder abuse Implications for research education and policy

[14] Understanding Elder Abuse in Family Practice by Dr. Mark J. Yaffe and Dr. Bachir Tazkarji

[15] © The Elder Abuse Suspicion Index (EASI) was granted copyright by the Canadian Intellectual Property Office (Industry Canada) February 21, 2006. (Registration # 1036459).

The EASI was developed* to raise a doctor's suspicion about elder abuse to a level at which it might be reasonable to propose a referral for further evaluation by social services, adult protective services, or equivalents. While all six questions should be asked, a response of "yes" on one or more of questions 2-6 may establish concern

[16] Yaffe MJ, Wolfson C, Lithwick M, Weiss D. (2008). Development and Validation of a Tool to Improve Physician Identification of Elder Abuse: The Elder Abuse Suspicion Index (EASI). Journal of Elder Abuse & Neglect. February 2008, 20(3), 276-300

[17] Canadian Centre for Elder Law, Report on Vulnerable Investors: Elder Abuse, Financial Exploitation, Undue Influence and Diminished Mental Capacity." British Columbia Law Institute, 2017.

[18] Pickering, Yefimova and Maxwell, in their research, concluded that a caregiver's stress is one of the explanations for elder abuse. - Pickering C, Yefimova M, Maxwell C. CAREGIVER STRESS THEORY MAY EXPLAIN ELDER ABUSE BUT NOT NEGLECT IN DEMENTIA FAMILY CAREGIVING. Innov Aging. 2018;2(Suppl 1):851. Published 2018 Nov 11

[19] Sightlines Project Special Report: Social Engagement: Chapter I: The Importance of Social Relationships for Longevity by Jialu L. Streeter, Sarah Raposo, and Hsiao-Wen Liao

[20] The Harvard Study of Adult Development is the longest study when in 1938 they decided to track the health of 268 Harvard Sophomores. The purpose of the study was to determine how to live healthy and happy lives. "The surprising finding is that our relationships and how happy we are in our relationships has a powerful influence on our health," said Robert Waldinger, director of the study, a psychiatrist at Massachusetts General Hospital and a professor of psychiatry at Harvard Medical School. "Taking care of your body is important but tending to your relationships is a form of self-care too. That, I think, is the revelation." Robert Waldinger's TED talk, titled "What Makes a Good Life? Lessons from the Longest Study on Happiness," in 2015 provides a great summary of the importance of social connectivity.

[21] Ahead of World Elder Abuse Awareness Day, 15 June 2019, AGE Platform Europe stressed that society fails to collectively recognize elder abuse as a violation of human rights because of "deeply rooted ageism that prevails in our societies"

[22] Butler, 1975, p. 35. This has been adopted by the World Health Organization where they define ageism as the stereotyping, prejudice, and discrimination towards people on the basis of age.

[23] Anne-Sophie Parent is Secretary General of AGE Platform Europe, an EU Network representing people aged 50 plus across the EU.

[24] Nelson, (2002, 2005), He wrote "It is odd that we live in a society that actively supports prejudice against a group to which we all hope to belong."

[25] Our aging population is growing and between 2010 and 2031 is the period that the baby boomers will all reach 65. According to Statistic Canada this group will represent between 23% -25% of the Canadian Population in 2031 and between 24%-28% in 2061. In May 2017, the results of the 2016 Census was released and it stated, "there are more seniors than children living in Canada – there were 5.9 million people aged 65 and older – just slightly more than the country's 5.8 million children under 14". For example, in Ottawa, it is expected that the senior

population will more than double over the next 20 years and is expected to account for 22 per cent of the City's population by 2031.

[26] Levy, Zonderman, Slade & Ferucci, 2002 where they found that those who had a more optimistic perception of aging lived longer than those that had a negative view to aging.

[27] Developing a Research Agenda to Combat Ageism by Sarah Raposo and Laura L. Carstensen

[28] Produced by NICE, National Institute for the Care of the Elderly, in collaboration with Dr. Mark Yaffee.

www.ingramcontent.com/pod-product-compliance
Lightning Source LLC
Chambersburg PA
CBHW071729090426
42738CB00011B/2433